"When reading the Prophets, on [...]
puzzling over Isaiah, 'How can I [...]
Fortunately, Peter Gentry meets us on the road and asks, 'Do you understand what you are reading?' Gentry ably guides us through this strange and foreign land."

> **Lindsay Kennedy,** assistant pastor, Calvary Chapel Bothell, Bothell, Washington; blogger, *My Digital Seminary*

"Gentry succeeds most admirably in his stated objective, which is to enable readers to read and understand the Prophets. And he does so in a way that is truly exemplary, employing a clear, concise, logically developed writing style that makes it relatively easy to probe this potentially difficult subject—the Old Testament prophetic literature. In short, the author demystifies the Hebrew prophets and successfully relates their writings also to hermeneutical issues facing the church today—all in the space of less than 150 pages. This book would serve as a helpful introduction for adult Bible studies as well as college-level courses on hermeneutics. Scholars teaching at higher academic levels too would benefit from Gentry's excellent pedagogical approach."

> **Ernst R. Wendland,** instructor, Lusaka Lutheran Seminary, Zambia; Internal Examiner, University of Zambia

"Having established a stellar reputation already through his many publications in Old Testament studies—especially in Septuagint and biblical theology—Gentry reflects broad expertise here in his treatment of prophetism as an institution and in the literary output of the canonical Prophets of the Hebrew Bible. This is more than 'just another book on the Prophets: their lives, times, and ministries.' The approach in this case goes beyond the standard of the *oeuvres* already at hand. Gentry knits together most skillfully the strands of criticism, theology, history, poetry, apocalyptic, and pastoral practicality in a style that betrays at once solid scholarship and transparent readability."

> **Eugene H. Merrill,** distinguished professor emeritus of Old Testament Studies, Dallas Theological Seminary

"When traveling to a foreign land, the experience is so much richer when you have an experienced guide to explain the unique customs, point out things you might have missed, and take you to places you would not dare traverse alone. For modern Western readers of the Bible, the Prophets are a foreign land, even if we do not initially realize it. Peter Gentry, with his decades of experience traveling in this difficult terrain, can be your expert guide to the biblical Prophets through reading this book. I'm overjoyed that Gentry is sharing in print for a wider audience what I first found so helpful as class lectures a dozen years ago. Pick up this travel guide and experience the biblical Prophets afresh."

Richard Lucas, Biblical and Theological Studies mentor, The NETS Center for Church Planting and Revitalization; associate pastor, Christ Memorial Church, Williston, Vermont

"Peter Gentry is a master exegete and theologian, and in this brief volume he supplies excellent guidance for those of us who desire to read and understand the Prophets with greater biblical faithfulness. With clear prose and numerous examples, he identifies how we should approach the prophetic genre—its grounding in the Mosaic covenant, its structure and use of repetition, its engagement of foreign nations, its use of typology and apocalyptic language, and its appropriation and already-but-not-yet fulfillment in the New Testament. Gentry helps us grasp how the prophets communicated their messages, and by doing so he empowers us to become better interpreters of God's Word. I highly recommend this book."

Jason S. DeRouchie, professor of Old Testament and biblical theology, Bethlehem College & Seminary

"Many people set out to read through the Bible but get bogged down in the Old Testament Prophets. Some push ahead anyway, others skip ahead—both missing out on the full counsel of God. But there's hope—everyone should read Peter Gentry's new book! Under seven key topics he asks the right questions, and his answers are the most insightful I've seen. Pastors and scholars: you'll benefit too."

Brent Sandy, former professor and chair of the Department of Religious Studies, Grace College, Winona Lake, IN; coeditor, *Cracking Old Testament Codes*; coauthor, *The Lost World of Scripture*; author, *Plowshares and Pruning Hooks*

How to Read and Understand

the Biblical Prophets

HOW TO READ AND UNDERSTAND THE BIBLICAL PROPHETS

PETER J. GENTRY

WHEATON, ILLINOIS

Library of Congress Cataloging-in-Publication Data

Names: Gentry, Peter John, author.
Title: How to read and understand the biblical prophets / Peter J. Gentry.
Description: Wheaton : Crossway, 2017. | Includes bibliographical references and index.
Identifiers: LCCN 2016035994 | ISBN 9781433554032 (tp) | ISBN 9781433554056 (mobi) | ISBN 9781433554063 (epub)
Subjects: LCSH: Bible. Prophets—Criticism, interpretation, etc. | Bible—Prophecies.
Classification: LCC BS1505.52 .G46 2017 | DDC 224/.06—dc23
LC record available at https://lccn.loc.gov/2016035994

VP		32	31	30	29	28	27	26	25	24	23	22
18	17	16	15	14	13	12	11	10	9	8	7	6

For C. B.
and my friends at DTS

Contents

Contents

Introduction

In our modern society of e-readers, many may have forgotten what a newspaper looks like. Yet hopefully we can all grasp the following illustration. When we pick up a newspaper from a big city, we find many sections. We expect to see the main headlines and news reports on the front page or in the first section. Later on we come to the entertainment section and find there the comics or funnies. Now, here's the question I want to ask you: can we say that we find truth on the front page and entertainment only in the comics?

The more we think about how to answer that question, the more we come to realize that there may, in fact, be more truth in terms of comment on family life, morals, political events, and current philosophical or social issues in the comics than we find on the front page. However, we can miss it because of what we expect to find in particular types of literature or genres. Consider the example from *Pearls Before Swine* by Stephan Pastis (p. 12).

We see in the Pastis comic how Rat completely misses the point of *Hagar the Horrible*, because the literary features he's looking at aren't the ones that really matter. We might hear him shouting, "But what about the literal interpretation of the text?" Intelligent Rat may even appeal to speech-act theory: "But Muqtada al-Sadr, the Shiite cleric, made a *promise*, and a promise is a promise!" Apparently not all readers in the Western world are able to comprehend comics. The cartoon author is concerned that many readers may not have the proper strategies for reading this kind of

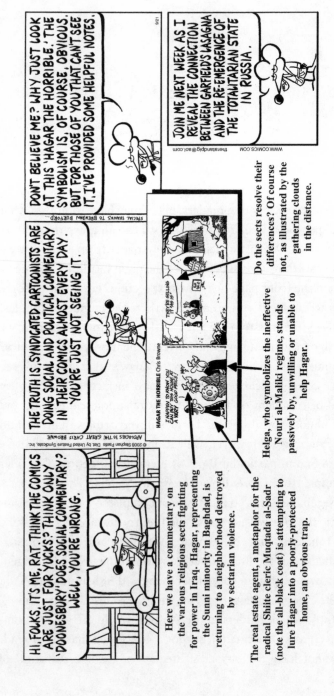

Here we have a commentary on the various religious sects fighting for power in Iraq. Hagar, representing the Sunni minority in Baghdad, is returning to a neighborhood destroyed by sectarian violence.

The real estate agent, a metaphor for the radical Shiite cleric Muqtada al-Sadr (note the all-black coat) is attempting to lure Hagar into a poorly-protected home, an obvious trap.

Helga, who symbolizes the ineffective Nouri al-Maliki regime, stands passively by, unwilling or unable to help Hagar.

Do the sects resolve their differences? Of course not, as illustrated by the gathering clouds in the distance.

* The author does not agree with the views of the cartoonist. Used for illustration purposes only.

literature. Since the comics are pictures, the authors communicate by heavy use of metaphors and symbols.

A lack of proper reading strategies is exactly the problem some have with reading the Bible. When I went to seminary in the 1970s, prior to the shift to postmodernism, the focus was on how to interpret the letters of Paul. But what kind of literary work is a "gospel"? What literary strategies or techniques do narrators or storytellers use to help the reader grasp their main points? And how do we read and understand the Hebrew prophets of the Old Testament? In one sense, prophecy is not a particular genre or type of literature, since the prophets use every possible genre and literary type to communicate their messages. Even more difficult to understand are prophecies such as Daniel, Zechariah, and Revelation, which are frequently described as "apocalyptic" literature.

A central problem in the Christian church, especially during the last one hundred years, is that we have been reading the Gospels of the New Testament, the narratives of the Old Testament and the book of Acts, and the Hebrew prophets of the Old Testament and the New Testament (e.g., Revelation), including apocalyptic prophecies, exactly the same way we read Romans. In addition to this, we support our interpretation by claiming that we are following a *literal* interpretation of Scripture. But every day as we read the pages of our newspapers (for those of us who still do), we don't even think about mentally switching gears as we turn from the front page to the comics.

We might well ask if the literature of the biblical prophets actually constitutes its own genre or type of literature, since the prophets use an extremely wide variety of speech types to communicate. They communicate by different kinds of disputation (Isa. 49:14–26) and judgment speeches (e.g., Isaiah 13; Jer. 4:5–8); by promises of restoration and salvation (Isa. 4:2–6; 11:1–9; 40:9–11); by allegories (Ezekiel 16; 31:2–9) and parables (Isa. 5:1–7); by lawsuit and legal speeches (Isa. 1:1–20; 41:1–7, 21–29); by biography (Jonah); and by funeral speeches (Isa. 29:1–10). Moreover, the prophets communicated not only by their words but also by symbolic acts, drama, and one-act plays. Jeremiah hid his underwear in a rock (Jer. 13:1–7). Isaiah went naked and barefoot for three years (Isa. 20:1–3). Ezekiel cut off his hair and then burned a third of it, struck a third with a sword, and cast a third to the wind (Ezek. 5:1–4). So how can we say that there is anything particularly characteristic of prophetic literature? How can we employ a method of literary study that attempts to affirm what is typical and not typical? Are there any principles that do apply to all the literature of the prophets?

Yes, there are! In this short work I lay out seven characteristics or features of prophetic literature in the Bible. Understanding and using these characteristics of the biblical prophets as reading strategies will help Christians comprehend these texts for themselves, perhaps for the first time with real understanding. You will have the cues the first readers had for reading these texts. Here are the topics taken up in these pages:

Exposing Covenant Disloyalty	Chapter 1
The Purpose of Announcing Future Events	Chapter 2
The Function of Repetition in Hebrew Literature	Chapter 3
Why So Many Speeches about Foreign Nations?	Chapter 4
Where the Past Becomes a Model for the Future	Chapter 5
Apocalyptic: The Use of Wild Metaphors and Symbols	Chapter 6
Chronology and Literature That Paint Panoramas	Chapter 7

It is not my purpose in these pages to push a particular brand of eschatology, i.e., what the Bible teaches about events in the future or at the end times. What I hope and pray is that this book will help *all* believers learn how to read and understand the texts of the biblical prophets on their own. They are a different kind of literature from Romans, as much so as comics differ from the front page of a newspaper. We need to spell out in detail the rules for reading this kind of literature if the church is going to understand these texts as the authors intended us to understand them.

1

Calling the People Back
to the Covenant

Everything in the prophets is based upon the covenant made between God and Israel during the exodus from Egypt, especially the expression or form of the covenant as it is found in the book of Deuteronomy. Claus Westermann, in his book *Basic Forms of Prophetic Speech*, demonstrates and details this in many ways.[1] For the prophets, their perspectives on social justice, their promises and their threats, *even their very sentences and words*, are all based upon the book of Deuteronomy, an expansion and renewal of the covenant made at Sinai.

> Covenant: an agreement between two parties
> making binding, official, and permanent a relationship
> of faithful, loyal love, obedience, and trust. Not a
> business contract or marketplace agreement.

---

1. Claus Westermann, *Basic Forms of Prophetic Speech*, trans. Hugh Clayton White (Louisville, KY: Westminster, 1991).

The Abrahamic covenant is foundational to the Mosaic/Israelite covenant in Deuteronomy, and the Davidic covenant is a further development in the sequence of covenants established by God. So the statement, "Everything in the prophets is based on the Mosaic covenant made at Sinai and renewed at Moab," is not intended to exclude prophetic statements that may be directly tied to the covenant at creation,[2] the covenant with Abraham, and the covenant with David. Nonetheless, the main concern of the prophets is Israel's relationship to Yahweh as defined by the Mosaic covenant.

As a covenant people, Israel was constantly flagging in her loyalty to Yahweh. Instead of being completely devoted to Yahweh (i.e., holy), they hedged their bets with Baal, the rain god, and other false gods used by humans to manipulate the powers that be; and instead of loving their neighbors as themselves, their lifestyle and society were filled with social injustice.

Illustration from Isaiah 5 and 6

Hebrew Literature

Isaiah 5 and 6 provide an excellent example of this business of "calling the people back to the covenant," and a detailed explanation of this section will help us illustrate this aspect of prophetic writing.

As we noted above, reading and studying the Bible may not be straightforward for readers with a *modern* and *Western* background in culture and language. The biblical texts in origin are *ancient* and *Eastern*—they come from a different culture and a different time. The normal pattern of Hebrew literature is to consider topics in a *recursive* manner, which means that a topic

---

2. In Gen. 1:26–27, the terms "image" and "likeness," according to the ancient Near Eastern background of the text, indicate a covenant relationship between God and humans, on the one hand, and between humans and the rest of the world, on the other. These relationships can be captured by the ideas of "obedient sonship" and "servant kingship," respectively. This is what is meant by a covenant at creation. See chap. 6 in Peter J. Gentry and Stephen J. Wellum, *Kingdom through Covenant: A Biblical-Theological Understanding of the Covenants* (Wheaton, IL: Crossway, 2012).

is progressively repeated. Such an approach seems monotonous to those who do not know and understand how these texts communicate.

Using the recursive approach, a Hebrew author begins a discourse on a particular topic, develops it from a particular perspective, and then concludes his conversation. Then he begins another conversation, taking up the *same topic again* from a different point of view. When these two conversations or discourses on the same topic are heard in succession, they are like the left and right speakers of a stereo system. Do the speakers of a stereo system give the same music, or do they give different music? The answer is that the music they give is *both* different *and* the same. In one sense the music from the left speaker is identical to that of the right, yet in another way it is slightly different so that the effect is stereo instead of just one-dimensional. Just so, in Hebrew literature the ideas presented can be experienced like 3-D Imax movies with Dolby surround sound—they are three-dimensional or full-orbed ideas.

This pattern in Hebrew literature functions on both macro and micro levels. Individual sentences are placed back-to-back like left and right speakers. Paragraphs and even larger sections of texts are treated the same way. There is a more detailed description in chapter 3, but in just a moment we will see the importance of grasping these literary patterns in the Hebrew Bible.

Literary Unity of Isaiah

Few scholars today treat the book of Isaiah as a literary unity. Methods of studying the text are heavily influenced by the rationalism of the Enlightenment period and focus on modern and Western literary approaches instead of ancient and Eastern rules for composing texts. As a result, most of the commentaries are focused on grammatical and lexical details of individual words and phrases, with the result that no larger picture of the book as a whole emerges from their labors.

For a hundred years or more, scholars have not asked, What were the Hebrews' own principles and rules for telling stories? And how did the authors of that culture and time construct their works? Yet if those questions are asked, it is possible to discern a central theme for the book of Isaiah as a whole and to divide the book into seven separate sections in which Isaiah goes around the same topic like a kaleidoscope, looking at it from different perspectives. The literary structure of each prophetic book as a whole is *fundamental to interpretation*.

Barry Webb is one scholar who has taken the unity of Isaiah seriously and has argued persuasively that the book as a whole centers on the theme of corruption and social injustice in the city of Jerusalem, or Zion, in the eighth century BC that results in divine judgment but ends with a vision of a future renewed and transformed Zion.[3]

Isaiah 1 details the idolatrous worldview gripping Jerusalem and the corruption in society resulting from it. The covenant made between God and Israel at Sinai (and expanded and renewed on the plains of Moab) describes curses and judgment on the people for violating the covenant. After the judgment, however, God will remake, renew, restore, and transform Zion, and Isaiah 2:1–4 envisions this future Zion as a mountain dwarfing all others and one to which all the nations will stream to receive instruction from Yahweh on behavior and lifestyle.

Then in chapters 3 and 4 Isaiah goes around the same topic again, indicting Jerusalem for social injustice and ending with a glorious vision of the future Zion. He depicts the road from judgment to a future city of Zion, which is characterized by righteousness, in the language of a new exodus. Just as God brought his people out of bondage in Egypt after 430 years, so he will bring

---

3. Barry G. Webb, "Zion in Transformation: A Literary Approach to Isaiah," in *The Bible in Three Dimensions: Essays in Celebration of Forty Years of Biblical Studies in the University of Sheffield*, ed. D. J. A. Clines, Stephen E. Fowl, and Stanley E. Porter, Journal for the Study of the Old Testament: Supplement Series 87 (Sheffield, UK: Sheffield Academic Press, 1990), 65–84. See also Barry G. Webb, *The Message of Isaiah: On Eagles' Wings* (Downers Grove, IL: InterVarsity Press, 1996).

them out of their slavery to sin and chronic covenant unfaithfulness into a brand-new creation and a community bound by a new covenant. This new exodus will be bigger and better than the first.

The next section runs from chapters 5 to 12 and begins to develop the same themes a third time in the context of a military and political crisis in Judah. Assyria, a sleeping giant, had awakened and was expanding westward toward Syria and then southward into Palestine. The countries of Syria (with its capital in Damascus) and the northern kingdom of Israel (with its capital in Samaria) were putting pressure on the little kingdom of Judah in the south to join them in an anti-Assyrian coalition. The plan of King Ahaz of Judah was to become a vassal or client-king of Tiglath Pileser III of Assyria (called "Pul" in the Bible) and appeal to Assyria to fend off his Israelite and Aramaean enemies to the North. This section also ends by focusing on a future Messiah—a coming King—and the new exodus, giving us a glorious vision of the new world and his rule there.

As we might expect, this third section, chapters 5–12, begins by developing further the accusations of the loss of social justice. We might also expect that by this time Isaiah's audience had had enough of his message. So this time, in order to make sure that his audience participates, Isaiah presents his message in the form of a parable. His approach to the audience is similar to how Nathan the prophet approached King David when the Lord sent him to the king to confront him about his adultery with Bathsheba and the murder of her husband, Uriah. There, too, Nathan used a parable to get audience participation from the king and thereby have David condemn himself (2 Sam. 12:1–6).

As we focus our attention on Isaiah 5, it is extremely important to observe the literary structure. Here we want to ask: In what form is this message given to us? In other words, what is the shape of the text? The arrangement and form or literary shape of the statements in the text are as important for interpretation of a communication as the meaning of the actual individual sentences.

Chart 1.1

Explanation of Isaiah 5

Outline or Structure of Isaiah 5:1–30

I.	Song of the Vineyard	5:1–7
	A. A Story of a Vineyard and Its Fruit	1–2
	B. The Listeners Asked for a Verdict	3–4
	C. The Decision of the Owner	5–6
	D. The Application to Judah	7
II.	Bad Grapes: Indictment of God's People	5:8–24
	A. Round 1	8–17
	1. Woe: Land Grabbing	8–10
	2. Woe: Partying and Revelry	11–12
	a. Therefore 1	13
	b. Therefore 2	14–17
	B. Round 2	18–24
	3. Woe: Mocking Divine Justice	18–19
	4. Woe: Inverting God's Standards	20
	5. Woe: Self-Approved Wisdom	21
	6. Woe: Partying and Inverting Social Justice	22–23
	a. Therefore 3	24
III.	The Vineyard Ravaged: Announcement of Punishment	5:25–30
	A. The Final Therefore	5:25

Chapter 5 is divided into three sections. The first is a parable or song about a vineyard, in verses 1–7. The second section goes from verses 8–24 and applies the parable to the people of Judah and Jerusalem in Isaiah's time. The last section describes the coming judgment: God will bring a distant nation to conquer and destroy them and their way of life.

The parable and its application. The "Song of the Vineyard" in the opening section can be briefly summarized. The parable is divided into four stanzas. The first stanza relates in song a story of a farmer preparing a vineyard and expecting good vintage. Instead, he is met by rotten, stunted grapes.[4] In the second stanza the listeners are asked for a verdict. The third part confirms the rhetorical question posed in the second stanza by relating the decision of the owner of the vineyard. He will do exactly as the listeners expect him to do—he will destroy this useless fruit orchard. Then comes the punch line of the parable, and what a great shock it is. The parable is applied to Judah and Jerusalem in the last stanza; they are the bad grapes!

Verses 8–24, which I have entitled "Bad Grapes," constitute a damning indictment of the people of God. A series of six woes details and specifies the bad grapes indicated in verses 2 and 4 of the parable. The literary structure is the clue to the meaning of the text. The key words are *woe* and *therefore*. *Woe* is a key word used to describe and identify the sins for which the people will be punished. *Therefore* is a key word used to detail the divine punishment for these specific sins. The punishment is based squarely upon retributive justice, since this is the main principle of the Torah (Genesis through Deuteronomy).

Notice, however, how these woes are presented. First there are two woes, in verse 8 and verse 11, which are followed by two therefores, in verses 13 and 14. Then there are a series of four more woes, in verses 18, 20, 21, and 22, given in staccato fashion like rapid gun shots. This is followed by another *therefore* in verse 24. The word *therefore* divides the woes into two groups; here Isaiah, in typical Hebrew literary style, is going around the topic twice from two different angles or points of view.

The section indicting the people of God is then followed by an announcement of imminent punishment. This last paragraph is introduced by a conjunction that also means "therefore," but the word in Hebrew is different because this is the big *therefore*

---

4. Nogah Hareuveni explains *beushim* (bad grapes) as a specific stage of development in the growth of the grapes, when they cease being embryonic but have not yet ripened. A disease called *zoteret* strikes vineyards and prevents grapes from ripening, leaving them in the stunted stage of *beushim*. This explanation is from Mishna *Ma'asrot* 1.2 and the Jerusalem Talmud. See Nogah Hareuveni, *Tree and Shrub in Our Biblical Heritage*, trans. Helen Frenkley (Israel: Neot Kedumim, 1984), 70–73.

that takes up the three little *therefores* in the previous verses (13, 14, 24).

Consequently the six woes are divided into two groups, two in the first group and four in the second. At the heart of all of them is the violation of social justice as is indicated by the last line of verse 7—the punch line of the parable—where we have the word pair *justice* and *righteousness* (hereafter *justice-righteousness*).

Now, according to the Hebrew poetry—which is based upon placing lines in parallel pairs—*justice* is matched in the first line by *righteousness* in the second. Normally in prose when the words *justice* and *righteousness* are joined together, they form a single concept or idea—best expressed in English by the term *social justice*. This is a figure of speech known as a "hendiadys," one concept expressed through two words. The word pair becomes an idiom expressing a single thought that is both different from and greater than the words considered independently. Just as one cannot analyze the expression "by and large" in English by studying *by* and *large* separately, so one cannot determine the meaning of this expression by analyzing *justice* and *righteousness* separately. Hebrew poetry, however, allows such a word pair to be split so that half is in one line of the couplet and the other half is in the parallel line. The word pair *justice-righteousness* is central to the discourse of Isaiah and occurs some eighteen times, always at critical or key points in the discourse.[5]

Bible scholars and religious leaders came to Jesus and asked him, "Which is the greatest commandment in the Law?" Similarly in the Old Testament, many years earlier, as Isaiah and the other prophets sought to apply the covenant with Moses and Israel to their situation and times, they found new ways to condense and

---

5. Some eighteen or nineteen instances of the word pair *justice-righteousness*, frequently split over poetic parallelism, occur in Isaiah: 1:21; 1:27; 5:7; 5:16; 9:6(7); 11:4; 16:5; 26:9; 28:17; 32:1, 32:16; 33:5; 51:5; 56:1; 58:2(2x); 59:4; 59:9; 59:14. In 11:4; 51:5; and 59:4, verbal forms of the root *judge* are employed instead of the noun *judgment*; the instance in 51:05 is not listed in the rather exhaustive and excellent study of Leclerc although it appears as valid as the instance in 11:4. See Thomas L. Leclerc, *Yahweh Is Exalted in Justice: Solidarity and Conflict in Isaiah* (Minneapolis: Fortress, 2001), esp. 10–13, 88, 157.

summarize in a single sentence or even a phrase the apparently unwieldy mass of commands and instructions in the Torah.[6] Even the Ten Words (Commandments) upon which some six hundred or so instructions are based could be further condensed and summarized. An example is the famous passage in Micah 6:8, "What does the LORD require of you but to do justice, and to love kindness, and to walk humbly with your God?" (ESV).

The heart of Isaiah's message is that the covenant between God and Israel given by Moses at Sinai is broken. He summarizes this covenant, consisting of the Ten Commandments and the Judgments in Exodus 20–23, using expressions or idioms for social justice and faithful, loyal love or being truthful in love. This can be described and illustrated from Isaiah's prophecy in 16:5 (NIV):

> In *love* a throne will be established;
>   in *faithfulness* a man will sit on it—
>   one from the house of David—
> one who in judging seeks *justice*
>   and speeds the cause of *righteousness*.

In contrast to the regime of the kings of Isaiah's time, a future king is promised who will rule in justice and righteousness. Again, as in Isaiah 5:7, we have the word pair split so that half is in one line of the couplet and half in the parallel line. Similarly, in the first half of the verse we have *love* in the first half of the couplet and *faithfulness* in the second half. This is another word pair that is focused on fulfilling one's obligations and doing what is right in a covenant relationship (such as marriage).

Now, Isaiah's promise of a future king in 16:5 is based upon Deuteronomy 17. Verses 16–20 of Deuteronomy 17 describe the manner in which the future king of Israel is to fulfill his responsibilities. Three negative commands in verses 16–17 are followed by three positive commands in verses 18–20, all relating to the Torah:

---

6. See Matt. 22:36–40.

(1) the king shall copy the Torah; (2) the king shall have the Torah with him; and (3) the king shall read the Torah.[7] In other words, the only positive requirement is that the king embody *torah* as a model citizen. This is exactly what Isaiah is saying in 16:5, only he employs the concept of social justice, expressed by the broken word pair *justice-righteousness* as a summary for the Torah. Deuteronomy calls for a king who implements the Torah in his regime, and Isaiah predicts a king who will deliver social justice in his rule. They are saying the same thing.

We should note in passing that the word *torah* is poorly translated by the English word *law*. Many Christians think of *torah* mainly as law, i.e., the law of Moses. Two important facts should shape our thinking about *torah*: first, the Hebrew word *tôrâ* means "direction" or "instruction," not "law"; second, these instructions are given in the form of a covenant, not a law treatise. The Torah, then, is unlike any law code in the ancient Near East or even today. It is a set of instructions for living, set in the context and framework of a covenant relationship. The Torah is God instructing his children as a father in a family or as a husband in a marriage relationship—a relationship of faithfulness, loyalty, love, trust, and obedience. It is not a code of laws or requirements that are imposed generally upon human society by an impersonal authority. Here I use the words *instruction* and *torah* interchangeably to try to keep these truths in focus.

The meaning of the word pair *justice-righteousness* both as an expression for social justice and as a summary of the instruction in the covenant is clearly illustrated, in particular in Isaiah 5, in the series of six woes divided into two separate conversations or groups. In verse 7, the word pair *justice-righteousness* broken or split over parallel lines is not only the punch line for the parable; it is also the headline for the next section, showing that the violation of social justice is at the heart of all six woes. In the first woe the

---

7. Cf. Daniel I. Block, "The Burden of Leadership: The Mosaic Paradigm of Kingship (Deut. 17:14–20)," *Bibliotheca Sacra* 162 (2005): 259–78.

prophet thunders about land grabbing: "Woe to those who add house to house and field to field" (v. 8). The second woe (v. 11) condemns the partying of those enjoying newfound wealth, because the money for these parties came from mistreating the poor and vulnerable. The final four woes are all ways of elaborating the original charge of perverting social justice. The last woe is the climax and summarizes by combining the two original charges of gaining wealth by social injustice and living a life of pleasure to spend that wealth. Between the two groups of woes Isaiah announces punishments based upon the retributive justice of the covenant/the Torah.

Further details explained. In the first round, as we have seen, the woe of verse 8 has to do with greedy grabbing of land, while the woe of verse 11 has to do with partying and revelry. Partying and revelry occupied the leisure time of the rich and resulted from the wealth generated by mistreating the poor and vulnerable.

In the second round, the last four woes are actually a repetition of the first two in recursive development of the topic. The third woe talks about the upper classes carrying a burden of sin bound by big ropes of deceit and mocking God by calling upon him to hurry up with the judgment that he has promised. The fourth woe shows that the system of virtue and vice, of right and wrong, is completely inverted in this society. The fifth woe accuses the people of depending on self-approved knowledge and skill. They are confident in and relying on their technology and mastery of the powers of nature. I remember well around 1979 when we first heard of the disease now called AIDS. The immediate attitude in North America was: "Just give us enough time and a better technology and we will beat this"—an example of relying on our own technology.

The woes, then, are all ways of elaborating the original charge of perverting social justice. The last woe is the climax and summarizes by combining the two original charges of gaining wealth by social injustice and living a life of pleasure to spend that wealth.[8] In this way the last four woes elaborate the original two indictments. These indictments and the punishments that result are based entirely upon the retributive justice of the Torah, the covenant made at Sinai. The penalty always exactly matches the crime. The wrongdoer must repay as much as but no more than the wrong done.

The economic and social situation addressed by Isaiah in chapter 5 signals the breakdown of conventions governing ownership of property.[9] Prior to the monarchic period, Israelite economy was based on farming and shepherding. Property was inherited and preserved within clans, a kin group between the extended family and the tribe. Diverse instructions in the Mosaic covenant were given to preserve economic equilibrium in ownership of property and to protect the poor and powerless, e.g., laws concerning boundary markers,[10] the inheritance rights of females,[11] levirate marriage,[12] duties and responsibilities of the nearest relative,[13] and jubilee/sabbatical years.[14] Two factors brought changes to the social system: monarchy and urbanization. With the advent of kingship, land could be acquired by the crown: sometimes corruptly as in the case of Naboth's vineyard (1 Kings 21) and sometimes legally through the confiscation of the estates of criminals and traitors. Thus, a family inheritance could be enlarged by a royal grant. Samuel warned about this in 1 Samuel 8:14–15. Recipients of such royal largesse would live in the capital city and eat every day at the king's table, while still enjoying the revenue of their amassed holdings. In this way, important nobles and officials,

---

8. Peter J. Gentry, "Sizemore Lecture I: Isaiah and Social Justice," *Midwestern Journal of Theology* 12 (2013): 1–16.

9. This description of the background to the social situation in Isaiah 5 is adapted from and based upon Leclerc, *Yahweh Is Exalted in Justice*, 59–60, who brings together many seminal studies on the topic.

10. Deut. 19:14; 27:17.

11. Num. 26:33; 27:1–11; 36:1–13.

12. Deut. 25:5–10; Ruth 4:5.

13. The duties of the nearest relative are: redemption of property (Lev. 25:23–28), of persons (25:47–55), of blood (Numbers 35), and of levirate marriage (Ruth 4:5, 10) by the nearest relative.

14. Leviticus 25.

especially those who ingratiated themselves with the king and his henchmen, were in a position to acquire by legal or illegal means the property of those vulnerable to oppression.[15]

On the other hand, the development and growth of cities created new ties between peasant farmers and a new class of merchants who usually lived in the towns and influenced public affairs. When a farmer suffered economic setbacks from crop failure due to drought or locusts, for example, he would turn to a merchant or moneylender in town. He would either be charged interest for a loan or be forced to cultivate land belonging to others on a sharecropping or tenant basis. We have documents from the Jewish community in Elephantine (Syene/Aswan), Egypt, from the fifth century BC that mention Jews who had to pay interest rates of 5 percent per month. When unpaid interest is added to the capital, the average annual rate is 60 percent.[16]

As agricultural plots become the property of a single owner (perhaps an absentee landlord who is a city dweller), as peasants become indentured serfs or even slaves, and as their goods and services are received as payments on loans, the gap between the rich and the poor widens. Since land ownership translates into economic and political power, issues of property rights and taxes, as well as laws concerning bankruptcy, foreclosures, and loans, fall into the hands of the rich, thus aiding and abetting a gap in power as well.

The situation that Isaiah condemns is graphically portrayed: large estates amassed by adding field to field on which sit "large and beautiful houses" (Isa. 5:9b ESV). The acquisition of land comes as debts are foreclosed and the property is expropriated. Since all this is done according to the laws of the marketplace and by statute, it is all strictly legal—but utterly immoral and in violation of the social justice of the Torah. This is a powerful demonstration of the parable of the vineyard at work: everything looks

---

15. Gentry, "Sizemore Lecture I," 1–16.
16. If one considers compounded (or unpaid) interest, the rate would be higher.

legal and proper on the outside, but on closer inspection shows that the grapes are rotten, stinking, and stunted. The image of a landowner dwelling all alone in the midst of the country is a picture of great horror. While American society idolizes and praises rugged individualism, ancient Israel valued the community over the individual. The interests of the group were more important than those of a single individual, no matter how clever or skilled and talented the entrepreneur. It is difficult, therefore, for us to feel the horror of ending up as a society of one.[17]

So the rich and luxuriant lifestyle of the upper class grows even as the poor get poorer. The punishment therefore fits the crime: the fine homes will become desolate and uninhabited (v. 9), and the fields so ravenously acquired will be blighted (v. 10). The same retribution is expressed in verse 17 when the prophet goes round the topic a second time.

The second woe describes the lifestyle of the growing upper class. The accumulated wealth frees the gentry, the landowners, from the necessity of working and allows them to enjoy a carefree and self-indulgent life. After the property and fine homes, the most conspicuous sign of this detached and carefree life is feasting and drinking—drinking literally from morning to night—which is twice decried (vv. 11, 22). Their fine feasts are accompanied by small orchestras—lyre and lute, tambourine and flute. Again, the punishment is directly matched to the offense. Verse 13 says, "Their nobility are poor wretches famished with hunger, and their multitude are parched with thirst."

The chapter ends without a shred of hope. In the last paragraph, God whistles to summon a distant nation that then brings across the desert a war machine so disciplined and powerful that there will be no escape. It reminds one of the troops of Sauron at the Gates of Mordor in *The Lord of the Rings*.

The literary structure is key to correct interpretation. The last

---

17. Gentry, "Sizemore Lecture I," 1–16.

four woes and the following *therefore* are an expansion upon the first two woes and the two climactic *therefores* that follow them. The literary structure, then, shows that verses 15 and 16 are both climactic and central as summaries of the condition of Israel and her situation before God:

> So humanity is humbled and mankind is brought low,
> and the eyes of the haughty will be brought low,
> but the Lord of Hosts is exalted in justice,
> and the Holy God shows himself holy in righteousness.[18]

Although the elite in Israel are enjoying the high life, they will be brought low and brought to recognize one who is truly exalted and high: Yahweh of Armies. He is exalted because he shows himself holy in justice and righteousness. The word pair for *social justice* split over parallel lines is found once more at this crucial juncture in the text, just as it was found in verse 7, the punch line of the parable.

What we can see in the biblical prophets, and in particular in Isaiah 5, is that God is bound to the nation of Israel by a covenant relationship. This covenant, made at Sinai, shows the people how to have a right relationship with God, how to treat one another in genuinely human ways, and how to be good stewards of the earth's resources.[19] *Social justice* is a term used by Isaiah and other prophets as a way of summarizing all the diverse instructions in the covenant. So here, the term *social justice* is defined by the detailed instructions in the covenant for treating other people in a genuinely human way.

In Isaiah 5, the prophet exposes the social injustice in Israel in their business dealings and announces the curses of the covenant and impending punishment based upon retributive justice. Thus the people are called back to the covenant relationship, and if they

---

18. Translation is that of H. G. M. Williamson, *A Critical and Exegetical Commentary on Isaiah 1–27* (New York: T&T Clark, 2006), 1:356–57.

19. See Gentry and Wellum, *Kingdom through Covenant*, passim.

do not return, they face certain destruction of their world as they know it.

Conclusion

What have we learned from our examination of Isaiah 5 and 6? The first and perhaps most important thing is that the biggest part of the message of the biblical prophets has nothing to do with predicting the future. This is extremely important to keep in mind since a large part of this little book deals with how and why the prophets predicted the future and what function that played in the message as a whole. Instead, the majority of what they had to say constitutes proclaiming a message that explains how the word of God, already revealed and received in the past, applies to present circumstances and situations. The promise or prediction that Israel would be exiled and judged for disobedience and disloyalty to the covenant did not require anything special beyond reading and preaching the book of Deuteronomy, given so long ago. And this is the largest part of the messages of the prophets.

2

The End of the Covenant, Judgment, and Restoration

As we are learning, one major purpose of the Old Testament prophets was to bring the people back to faithful love and loyalty to Yahweh in the covenant relationship established at Sinai (Exodus 19–24) and renewed at Moab (Deuteronomy). Was their ministry a success? By and large, no! This fact leads to important questions closely connected to the lack of real repentance and covenant faithfulness on the part of Israel. In particular, two questions come to mind: (1) Why were the words of the earlier prophets not put into writing as were the words of the later prophets? and (2) Why do we find astounding predictions concerning the future in the writings of the biblical prophets?

The Role of Future Predictions in the Old Testament Prophets

First, why were the words of the so-called major prophets (e.g., Isaiah, Jeremiah, and Ezekiel) recorded in writing? Many prophets had ministered since the time of Samuel, including great prophets like Elijah and Elisha. Frequently we consider Isaiah as one of the greatest prophets, but in the transfiguration, it is Moses and

Elijah who are talking with Jesus, not Moses and Isaiah. Yet we have nothing in writing attributed directly to Elijah. So why were the words of the earlier prophets not written down while those of the later prophets were? The answer is that a breaking point was reached in the covenant relationship between Yahweh and Israel.

Earlier prophets called the people back to the covenant, but when the people failed to return to the Lord, later prophets announced that the covenant or marriage relationship between Yahweh and Israel was virtually at an end, and therefore God would keep his curses and threats of judgment and punishment. He would also, however, eventually bring about the restoration of his people.

How many of us have gone to a grocery store and observed a mother saying to an unruly child for the tenth time, "If you do that again, I'll . . ." If we keep repeating our threats but don't act on them, we become foolish in the eyes of others. Our promises and threats become meaningless. At some point we have to act on our threats.

The circumstances in the covenant relationship between Yahweh and Israel necessitated future predictions and also required that the messages of the prophets be written down so as to establish the faithfulness of the Lord. There are, in fact, a number of reasons for foretelling the future in the biblical prophets' writings, and these are summarized below.

Distinguishing the True God from False Gods

First, prediction of the future distinguished Yahweh from the idols worshiped by the nations surrounding Israel and by faithless Israelites. The covenant relationship between Israel and Yahweh is summarized by two requirements or stipulations: (1) love God, and (2) love your neighbor as yourself. As we noted earlier, Israel's covenant violation was evidenced by idolatry (devotion to other gods) and social injustice. Rather than considering the interests of their neighbor and seeking to help others, they were taking advantage of the weaker members of society.

Isaiah in particular seeks to discredit the false gods and idols worshiped by Israel by proving that they are not gods. This is the focus of Isaiah 40–48. The one and only test that proves deity is the ability to both predict and, in fact, control the future. This test remains true today. No advances in our society in science and technology have enabled us to predict the future. This is why The Weather Channel is the most watched television network in America. We all want to know the future, and yet no one knows for sure how to predict and certainly cannot control future events.

Validation of the prophet. No one since Moses has had a direct hotline to heaven. During the rebellion against the leadership of Moses in Numbers 12, communication between God and Israel was clearly spelled out:

> And he [Yahweh] said, "Hear my words: If there is a prophet among you, I the LORD make myself known to him in a vision; I speak with him in a dream. Not so with my servant Moses. He is faithful in all my house. With him I speak mouth to mouth, clearly, and not in riddles, and he beholds the form of the LORD. Why then were you not afraid to speak against my servant Moses?" (vv. 6–8 ESV)

God spoke to Moses "mouth to mouth." All communication from God given apart from Moses would come through prophets in dreams and visions. This is described in detail in Deuteronomy 18, when Moses is about to die, and Moses makes absolutely clear how Israel may or may not know the divine will after his death. First, in Deuteronomy 18:9–13, Moses shows wrong ways to try to determine the will of God: resorting to mediums, people who practice divination or tell fortunes, those who inquire of the dead for guidance, those who interpret omens to make decisions, and those who engage in sorcery and witchcraft. These methods were commonly used by the nations surrounding Israel as ways of trying to determine the future and find the best plan of action.

But in Deuteronomy 18:14–22, Moses shows the right way

to know the will of God. God would raise up individuals, called prophets, from within the ethnic nation of Israel. The prophets would make known the divine will for both individuals and for the nation of Israel as a whole. Two tests were given for distinguishing a false prophet from a true prophet: (1) The true prophet must speak in the name of Yahweh, and those speaking in the name of other gods must be put to death. (2) If what a prophet predicted came to pass, he was a true prophet. If not, he was a false prophet and had spoken presumptuously.

One reason the biblical prophets gave predictions was to demonstrate publicly that only Yahweh knows and determines future events, and such demonstrations required a proper, scientific method. Predictions given concerning the future were made known publicly and *written down* at a specific date and time and attested publicly or verified by witnesses. Later on, when these predictions came true, people would see that Yahweh is indeed able to predict and determine the future.

Verifying predictions of the future. So we note that the predictions were to be given in a method that is sound, or even scientific, so to speak. How does this work? Normally in books like Isaiah, Jeremiah, Ezekiel, Daniel, and Zechariah, to mention some of the larger works, the prophet made predictions about events that would happen in two years or ten years—sometime in the *near* future, in the prophet's own time. When these predictions came true, the prophet was then validated in his community as one speaking for Yahweh and was thus known to be a true prophet. Therefore, when this same prophet spoke about events to happen in the *distant* future, or at some unknown or unspecified point in the future, his hearers could believe that he was indeed speaking for Yahweh, and Yahweh would be attested as the one and only true God against all idols and rivals.

In earlier parts of Isaiah, the prophet gives predictions of things that would happen shortly. For example, he predicts the coming of the Assyrians, who will bring destruction upon Judah as a form of divine judgment. Isaiah describes the attack like a big river in flood (Isa. 8:7–8), saying that the flood would come only to the neck, meaning that God would preserve Jerusalem. Later, in chapters 36–37, a messenger of Yahweh destroys 185,000 Assyrian soldiers, and King Sennacherib goes home without complete victory over Judah and Jerusalem. This validated Isaiah as a true prophet in the eyes of his contemporaries. So, later, when we read not only that God's people will be exiled from their homeland as the agreed-upon punishment for covenant violation but that someone named Cyrus would at a later date release the people of Judah from captivity, Isaiah's hearers should also believe this prediction, even though it may be far in the future. Here are Isaiah's own words:

> Who declared it from the beginning, that we might know,
>   and beforehand, that we might say, "He is right"?
> There was none who declared it, none who proclaimed,
>   none who heard your words. (Isa. 41:26 ESV)

> Behold, the former things have come to pass,
>   and new things I now declare;
> before they spring forth
>   I tell you of them. (Isa. 42:9 ESV)

> Thus says the LORD, your Redeemer,
>   who formed you from the womb:
> "I am the LORD, who made all things,
>   who alone stretched out the heavens,
>   who spread out the earth by myself,
> who frustrates the signs of liars
>   and makes fools of diviners,
> who turns wise men back
>   and makes their knowledge foolish,
> who confirms the word of his servant
>   and fulfills the counsel of his messengers,
> who says of Jerusalem, 'She shall be inhabited,'

> and of the cities of Judah, 'They shall be built,
>   and I will raise up their ruins';
> who says to the deep, 'Be dry;
>   I will dry up your rivers';
> who says of Cyrus, 'He is my shepherd,
>   and he shall fulfill all my purpose';
> saying of Jerusalem, 'She shall be built,'
>   and of the temple, 'Your foundation shall be laid.'"
>   (Isa. 44:24–28 ESV)

> Remember this and stand firm,
>   recall it to mind, you transgressors,
>   remember the former things of old;
> for I am God, and there is no other;
>   I am God, and there is none like me,
> declaring the end from the beginning
>   and from ancient times things not yet done,
> saying, 'My counsel shall stand,
>   and I will accomplish all my purpose,'
> calling a bird of prey from the east,
>   the man of my counsel from a far country.
> I have spoken, and I will bring it to pass;
>   I have purposed, and I will do it. (Isa. 46:8–11 ESV)

Just as God foretold to Abraham the enslavement in Egypt and subsequent exodus from Egypt four hundred years later (Gen. 15:13–16), so now, through Isaiah, he announces a bigger and better event: his people will be exiled in Babylon and later released, with Jerusalem and the temple being rebuilt. This is the difference between the former things and the new things. Isaiah's prediction is astounding! The superpowers of Isaiah's world were Assyria/Babylonia in the east and Egypt in the west. Cyrus was from Persia, a land of no significance in the eighth century BC, when Isaiah lived and prophesied. Today, with the superpowers being China and the United States, it would be like announcing a deliverer to come from Liechtenstein, a country of no international significance. Isaiah wrote down the prediction he had announced so that, later on, people could see that Yahweh both knows and determines the future. He alone is God, as Isaiah 46:9 concludes.

Explaining the Exile for Later Generations

Second, prediction of the future was necessary to explain the exile. Without the messages of the prophets, the people might have concluded that the gods of the nations were more powerful than Yahweh, which was why they had been captured and taken away into exile by these nations. This wrong belief is clearly illustrated in Isaiah 36:16–20 and 37:1–13. During that time period, the Assyrians attacked Judah and Jerusalem and conquered most of the cities in Judah. Today we have the documents and records from the king of Assyria, which were uncovered by archaeologists. The Annals of Sennacherib were recorded on a clay prism on which the Assyrian king states:

> As for Hezekiah, the Judean, I besieged forty-six of his fortified walled cities and surrounding smaller towns, which were without number. Using packed-down ramps and applying battering rams, infantry attacks by mines, breeches and siege machines, I conquered [them]. I took out 200,150 people, young and old, male and female, horses, mules, donkeys, camels, cattle, and sheep. He himself I locked up in Jerusalem, his royal city, like a bird in a cage. I surrounded him with earthworks and made it unthinkable for him to exit by the city gate.[1]

In Isaiah 36 and 37 the commander general of the Assyrian army, Rabshakeh, gives a message to the people in Jerusalem telling them not to trust in Yahweh and not to let King Hezekiah deceive them by telling them that Yahweh will deliver Jerusalem. The Rabshakeh gives a list of countries that Assyria has conquered and demonstrates that the gods of those conquered places had

---

1. Mordecai Cogan, "Sennacherib's Siege of Jerusalem (2.119B)," in *The Context of Scripture*, ed. William W. Hallo and K. Lawson Younger Jr. (Leiden, NL: Brill, 2003), 2:303.

been unable to deliver their people. Then Rabshakeh insults and mocks Yahweh, saying that he is no different from the gods of the conquered nations and will not be able to deliver Judah and Jerusalem. The gods of Assyria are bigger and better than Yahweh, Rabshakeh claims. According to Deuteronomy 32:27, this is exactly what Yahweh said the enemies would think.

Apart from the prophetic word, imagine what the people of Jerusalem would have thought when the Babylonians came and conquered the city and razed it to the ground, exiling the citizens to Babylon. Imagine undertaking the journey on foot, in chains for weeks, perhaps months, and finally arriving in Babylon in a land far away from home. Imagine walking down a corridor of high walls, beautifully decorated, and arriving at the massive Ishtar Gate of the city of Babylon. Archaeologists have reconstructed this gate, and it is displayed in a museum in Berlin. Even today, simply viewing the reconstruction is an overwhelming experience. Were it not for the prophetic word, the people of Judah and Jerusalem would surely have concluded: "Now we know why the Babylonians conquered us. It is because the gods of Babylon are bigger and more powerful than Yahweh."

Such a conclusion, of course, would have been utterly wrong. They were conquered for only one reason: they had violated the covenant, and the covenant curses of Deuteronomy 28 had come upon them. God had promised that he would send enemies and kick them out of their land, and he had finally kept his word and done it. God brought the Assyrians and the Babylonians against his own people for violating the covenant. It was necessary, then, for the predictions of Isaiah, Jeremiah, and Ezekiel to be written down so that when those events occurred, the people of Israel would draw the right conclusions.

Deliverance Takes Time

Third, the prediction of the future points to the fact that deliverance would take time, which is another reason why certain prophets wrote down their prophecies. There would be no quick fix in Isaiah's lifetime. Isaiah shows that the return of the people to a right relationship to Yahweh would happen in two stages. First the people would be released from physical exile in Babylon. Second, the people would be released from spiritual exile and slavery to sin. The first return, physical release from Babylon, would take seventy years, according to Jeremiah. For roughly 490 years the people had neglected to give the land its sabbaticals, allotted periods of rest. Therefore, the people would remain exiled and the land would have its rest for seventy years, one sabbatical for each seven years (Jeremiah 25). Then another seventy sabbaticals (490 years) were set to deal with their rebellion and sin and incorrigible covenant disloyalty (Dan. 9:24). Finally, with the coming of the Messiah, Yahweh would circumcise the hearts of his people and make a new covenant in which the people would respond in faith to Yahweh's faithfulness to them. They would receive the forgiveness of sins. The temple would be rebuilt, and God would once more return to live in the midst of his people as king. The messages of the prophets were written down in order to bring great comfort and encouragement during the long, weary years while God worked out his purposes and plan of salvation.

Yahweh Is Sovereign

Fourth, prediction of the future demonstrates the sovereignty of Yahweh over the nations. Not only did the people of Judah and Jerusalem need to see demonstrated and proven that Yahweh knows and predicts the future, but the nations needed to see it as well. The Assyrians, for example, needed to know that it was not their military might and strategy that brought the downfall of Israel. It was due solely to Israel's sin and covenant violation. The Assyrians were simply instruments in the hands of a God who is sovereign over *all* the nations. Not just Israel, but all the surrounding nations too, had to see that Yahweh is the only true God and that any other so-called gods are really just no-names and nothings, not worthy of worship by humans.

The Word of Yahweh Is Trustworthy

Fifth, prediction of the future proves the trustworthiness of the word of Yahweh. Hence his people should believe his promises and his threats in the covenant. He, above all, is a faithful covenant partner. Isaiah 28–37 is all about whether the people will believe and trust the word of Yahweh.

The covenant is like a marriage relationship. How can two people continue in an intimate relationship of love when one does not believe or trust anything the other says? Lack of trust leads to the complete breakdown of such a relationship. In the same way, only when the people came to believe and rely upon the word of Yahweh, no matter how unlikely it might seem—a deliverer will come from Liechtenstein—could God and Israel have a covenant relationship of love, of faithfulness and loyalty, of obedience and trust. The prophets wrote down their messages as proof of the reliability of the word of Yahweh for later generations who would eventually be part of the renewal of the covenant relationship.

So there are many different reasons for the prophets to predict the future. That is why there is a wide variety of predictions, and different ways to describe the future, as we shall soon see. Nonetheless, it is fundamental that we see prediction of the future *as integral to the focus on calling Israel to account for covenant violation* since idolatry is at the heart of covenant violation, and the only distinction between false gods and Yahweh is the ability to announce and control the future.

3

The Function of Repetition
in Hebrew Literature

As noted at the outset, reading and studying the Bible, especially the Old Testament prophets, may not be straightforward for readers with a *modern* and *Western* background in culture and language. The biblical texts are *ancient* and *Eastern* in origin—they come from a different culture and a different time. Critical scholarship of the nineteenth and twentieth centuries did not rigorously ask these questions: What were the Hebrews' own rules for writing literature and prophecy? What patterns, rules, or traits did they use in their writing? Instead, analysis of the prophets as literature was based on *modern* and *Western* rules of literary analysis rather than the rules of literature governing *ancient* and *Eastern* texts.

The Nature of Hebrew Literature

We all know that Hebrew writers, including the prophets, were very repetitive. In fact, repetition is at the heart of Hebrew discourse. The normal pattern in Hebrew literature is to consider topics in a *recursive*—in other words, *progressively* repetitive—manner. This approach is boring, frustrating, and monotonous to those who do not know and understand that this approach was a purposeful way of communicating the content.

Normally a Hebrew writer would begin a discourse on a particular topic, develop it from a particular angle or perspective, and end by closing down that conversation. Then he would begin another conversation, taking up the *same topic again* from a different angle or point of view and considering it from a different perspective. Do you recall the illustration we considered earlier about stereo sound? When two conversations or discourses on the same topic are heard or read in succession, they are meant to function like the left and right speakers of a stereo system. Now, here is the key question: Do both speakers of a stereo system provide the *same* music or does each give *different* music? The answer is both—the music is different *and* the same. In one sense the music from the left speaker is identical to that of the right, yet in another way it is slightly different so that when we hear the two together, the effect is stereo instead of just one-dimensional or monaural. In Hebrew literature the ideas presented can be experienced in a similar manner.

Such an approach is completely opposite to scientific writing in our culture, which is based on our Greek and Roman heritage, going back especially to Aristotle. In our culture, a writer, perhaps a philosopher or scientist, begins at a certain point A, and he moves slowly in a direct line using arguments, evidence, and logic to point B.

The recursive approach in Hebrew literature—aimed at developing ideas in a three-dimensional manner, so to speak—is followed in any genre and even across genres, whether prose or poetry, *and* at both the micro and macro levels. Let me first illustrate from Exodus 19:5–6, where Yahweh announces his purpose for making the covenant at Sinai. He says to Israel:

> You will be my special treasure more than/out of all the nations . . . *and* you will be for me a kingdom of priests and a holy nation.

Two clauses or sentences are joined by the conjunction and constitute the declaration by Yahweh. The first is "You will be my special treasure more than/out of all the nations, for the whole earth is mine" (v. 5). The second is *"and* you will be for me a kingdom of priests and a holy nation" (v. 6).

If we begin with the second sentence, verse 6, notice that there are two phrases, "kingdom of priests" and "holy nation," also joined by "and." These two phrases are like the left and right speakers of a stereo system. A holy nation is a nation completely *devoted* to loving God and serving him. A kingdom of priests is a group of priests exhibiting the rule of God and in their ministry bringing others to experience God's rule in their lives—bringing others to *devote* themselves to the worship of God. Both phrases then, each in a slightly different way, speak of a group of people completely devoted to serving and worshiping God. The phrase "special treasure" is used in ancient Near Eastern literature and in the Old Testament of a king who is completely devoted to serving and worshiping his god or of an obedient son who is devoted to the service of his father.

In this way the two expressions or phrases in verse 6 are also like the left and right speakers of a stereo system, saying the same thing. Verse 6, in turn, is also the right speaker in relation to verse 5, because both verses speak of Israel's relation to Yahweh as a devoted and obedient son, serving and worshiping him.[1] We can see, then, that the approach is both repetitive and recursive. First, the two verses serve as a left and a right speaker. Second, *within* the second verse there is another left and right speaker.

We see this phenomenon across genres: Exodus 14 and 15 give first a prose and then a poetic account of crossing the Red Sea; Judges 4 and 5 give first a prose and then a poetic account of the destruction of Sisera and his Panzer division of iron chariots. Genesis 1:1–2:3 and 2:4–3:24 show the phenomenon within the

---

1. Peter J. Gentry and Stephen J. Wellum, *Kingdom through Covenant: A Biblical-Theological Understanding of the Covenants* (Wheaton, IL: Crossway, 2012), 315–27.

genre of narrative. Those narratives of the creation story were not composed from different sources, as scholars have mistakenly proposed from the eighteenth century onward; what we find in those accounts is the chief characteristic and method of how a *single author* communicates.

Poetry in Hebrew

This explanation of ancient Hebrew literature also accounts for the fact that almost all Hebrew poetry is based on the couplet, the *minimum version* of the left and right speakers to create a stereo or three-dimensional idea. The first line of the couplet represents the right speaker, and the second line represents the left. Occasionally authors follow patterns of threes, giving us *tricola* or triplets of discussions in discourse or in lines of poetry. Examples of triplets are not hard to find. In Isaiah 7–12 there are three panels or sections portraying the future king (7:10–17; 9:1–7; 11:1–9), and in Isaiah 49–53 there are three songs about the servant of Yahweh (49:1–13; 50:4–11; 52:13–53:12). A fourth song (42:1–9), however, dealing with the servant of Yahweh, is separated from the other three and placed much earlier in an introductory section.

As a way to illustrate, I simply opened the book of Isaiah in an entirely random way, and the first thing I saw was a couplet:

> Then sheep will graze as in their own pasture;
>   lambs will feed among the ruins of the rich. (5:17 NIV)

We can see that the second line of the couplet matches the first, but it also adds something: what the sheep can call "their own pasture" turns out to be the "ruins of the rich." Isaiah is announcing a coming judgment. Foreign nations will attack and leave the land in ruins. Those who are rich will suffer as much or even more than those who are poor. Those left behind will benefit from the ruins left by the rich. So both lines are saying the same thing, but when one puts the left and right speakers together, an idea that is greater than each of the individual lines results—a full-orbed idea, so to speak.

As I checked the ESV and the NIV to find how I should cite this text, I immediately noted a difference. The NIV translates "lambs" in the second line, whereas the ESV translates "nomads." Therefore, we have a minor problem. The word in the Hebrew text literally means "sojourners," those who come from one country to live in another. The translators of the ESV understood these to be desert nomads, while those of the NIV considered that in light of the parallelism, those from a different country were simply animals such as goats and sheep, which were driven from place to place in search of grazing pastures, like the flocks owned by Abraham. The difference in interpretation is not serious, but understanding the literary patterns used by the Hebrews does play a role in translating and understanding the text.

Word Pairs in Hebrew

If you recall, earlier we noted that there is a unit in Hebrew literature, smaller than the couplet in poetry, that functions in the same way—like the left and right speakers of a stereo system—called a "word pair." In word pairs, which are common in the Old Testament, two words are joined together with the conjunction *and*, and together the two words mean something different and also greater than either of the words alone. An example is the word pair *kindness-faithfulness*, which is found in Genesis 47:29–30:

> When the time drew near for Israel to die, he called for his son Joseph and said to him, "If I have found favor in your eyes, put your hand under my thigh and promise that you will show me kindness and faithfulness. Do not bury me in Egypt, but when I rest with my fathers, carry me out of Egypt and bury me where they are buried."
> "I will do as you say," he said. (NIV)

Jacob, also called "Israel," is asking his son Joseph to bury him in Canaan and not in Egypt. In the Old Testament, family relationships were covenantal, and that was the case here with father and son. There was an obligation on the part of the stronger party, Joseph, to help the weaker party, Jacob, and fulfilling this obligation is referred to here as showing kindness and faithfulness. The Hebrew of this particular word pair, *ḥesed* and *'ĕmet*, is used consistently in the Old Testament to describe a covenant relationship. Neither word has a convenient or simple equivalent in English. The first Hebrew word, *ḥesed*, has to do with showing kindness in loyal love. The second, *'ĕmet*, can be translated by either "faithfulness" or "truth." As a word pair, we cannot easily reduce the meaning of the whole to the sum of its constituent parts, just as we cannot explain the meaning of the phrase "odds and ends" by considering separately the words *odd* and *end*. This word pair operates, then, within covenant relationships and has to do with demonstrating faithful, loyal love within the covenant context.

A word pair, then, is a mini stereo sound bite in which two words, like the left and right speakers of the stereo, communicate an idea that is fuller and greater than either of the two words considered individually.

Chiasm in Hebrew Literature

This pattern of word pairs in Hebrew literature functions on both the macro and the micro level. Individual sentences are placed back-to-back like left and right speakers. Paragraphs and even larger sections of texts are treated the same way. If a speaker or writer wanted to communicate two or three different topics and repeat each topic twice, he could simply go through each one two times: A B C :: A´ B´ C´. But he could also arrange them in other ways, such as A B C :: C´ B´ A´. This second arrangement is called a "chiasm." The word *chiasm* comes from the letter in the Greek alphabet known as *chi* (χ), which is shaped like an X, where the top half of the letter is mirrored in the bottom half. If an author has three topics and repeats each one twice in the pattern A B C :: C′ B′ A′, the second cycle or repetition is a mirror image of the first arrangement or ordering of the three topics.[2]

A nice example is found in Isaiah 6:10, where Yahweh explains what will happen during Isaiah's long ministry of preaching:

> Make the heart of this people dull,
>> and their ears heavy,
>> and blind their eyes;
> lest they see with their eyes,
>> and hear with their ears,
>> and understand with their hearts,
>> and turn and be healed. (ESV)

Notice in the first half of the verse the progression from *heart* to *ears* to *eyes*. Then in the second half, the progression is reversed in mirror image, going from *eyes* to *ears* to *heart*. This is the pattern A B C :: C′ B′ A′.

Another chiastic structure is found in Isaiah 33:13–24, one of many sections in the book of Isaiah where the prophet describes the character and nature of the future transformed Zion—both the physical city and the people who live there:

A The People of the New Zion		13–16
B Zion's King: Land Possessed, Enemies Gone		17–19
C Zion's Safety and Security		20
B′ Zion's King: Land Possessed, Enemies Gone		21–23
A′ The People of the New Zion		24

---

2. See H. C. Brichto, *Toward a Grammar of Biblical Poetics* (New York: Oxford University Press, 1992), 13–14, 75–76, 86, 118, and 165; Victor M. Wilson, *Divine Symmetries: The Art of Biblical Rhetoric* (Lanham, MD: University Press of America, 1997); M. H. Woudstra, *The Book of Joshua*, New International Commentary on the Old Testament (Grand Rapids, MI: Eerdmans, 1981), 78; and esp. Charles Lock, "Some Words after Chiasmus," in John Breck, *The Shape of Biblical Language: Chiasmus in the Scriptures and Beyond* (Crestwood, NY: St. Vladimir's Seminary Press, 1994), 361–67. Also significant is Mary Douglas, *Thinking in Circles: An Essay on Ring Composition* (New Haven, CT: Yale University Press, 2007). None of these scholars seems to connect the repetitive character just described with the propensity for chiasm in Hebrew literary structures.

Now consider the passage in full to see whether the outline correctly matches the content in Isaiah:

Hear, you who are far away, what I have done;
    and you who are near, acknowledge my power.
Sinners in Zion are in dread;
    trembling has seized the godless:
"Who among us can dwell with a consuming fire?
    Who among us can dwell with everlasting blazes?"
He who walks righteously and speaks uprightly,
    who refuses gain from oppression,
who shakes his hands without accepting a bribe,
    who closes his ears from hearing about bloodshed
    and shuts his eyes from enjoying a look at evil,
he will dwell on the heights;
    his unassailable bunker will be a fortress high in rocky
        crags;
    his bread will be given him; his water supply will be sure.

Your eyes will behold the king in his beauty;
    they will see a land large in all directions.
Your heart will muse on calamity in the past:
    "Where is he who counted, where is he who weighed the
        tribute?
    Where is he who counted the towers?"
You will see no more an insolent people,
    a people of obscure speech that you cannot comprehend,
    in a mocking tongue that you cannot understand.
Behold Zion, the city of our appointed feasts!
    Your eyes will see Jerusalem,
    a place to live without worry, an immovable tent,
whose stakes will never be pulled up,
    nor will any of its cords be snapped.
But there the LORD will be mighty for us
    a place of broad rivers and streams,
where no galley with oars can go,

nor majestic ship can pass.
For the LORD is our judge; the LORD is our lawgiver;
the LORD is our king; he will save us.

Your tent cords hang loose;
they cannot hold the main pole in its place
or keep the canvas spread out.
Then prey and spoil in abundance will be divided;
even the lame will take the prey.
And no inhabitant will say, "I am sick";
the people who dwell there will be forgiven their iniquity.

Verses 13–16 call out to those far away (i.e., people from nations far off) and to those who are near (people in Israel, especially those who have put their trust in alliances with other nations in hopes of being delivered from the attack of the Assyrians). God is portrayed here as a consuming fire, because that is how he revealed himself to Israel when the Mosaic covenant was made. First Yahweh appeared to Moses in a burning bush (Exodus 3); then he appeared on Mount Sinai in fire and smoke (Exodus 19). Afterward and during every day of their travels through the desert to Canaan, the land promised to them, Yahweh appeared as a pillar of fire by night and a column of cloud/smoke by day (Ex. 13:21–22; Num. 14:14). Fire is an excellent image or metaphor, since it can bring either great benefits or great destruction.

Who can live with this fire? Isaiah cites phrases from Psalms 15 and 24 to show that only those characterized by justice and righteousness can do so. *Justice-righteousness* is another word pair, and it means "social justice." This social justice, however, is not what is meant by that term in America today; rather, it is a way of summing up all the commands in the Mosaic covenant for the right way to relate to God and to treat other people and the earth's resources.

Isaiah 33:17–19 speaks of a king who is beautiful (because his reign entails social justice) and a land spacious and wide in all directions. This land is completely free from Assyrian overlords who come and demand tribute and taxes.

Verse 20 focuses on the future stability and security of the future Jerusalem, the new Zion. Unlike a nomadic tent, which is pulled down and set up as the nomads move from place to place looking for good pasture, Jerusalem will be an immovable tent.

Verses 21–23 speak more clearly about the king than verses 17–19 do. The beauty of the king lies in both the deliverance and the rule brought about by Yahweh. These verses, like 17–19, also speak of the enemies gone. In the book of Isaiah, those who travel in ships represent the foreign nations that were either sought for alliances or unsought as attackers and destroyers. The image here is not that of a ship, as some translations render, but rather of a tent about to fall down. It refers to the tent of the Assyrians who attacked in 701 BC.

Finally, verse 24 speaks again of the people, healed physically and forgiven for breaking their covenant relationship with God. So the last section matches the first, and the fourth section matches the second. In the center is the picture of a future city of God, firm and stable forever.

There is a theological problem, however, in this text. Verses 13–16 seem to say that only the righteous can dwell in God's presence; only those characterized by social justice in their behavior can live in the future Zion. Is Isaiah preaching salvation by works? What we must do is read verses 13–16 as the left speaker and verse 24 as the right speaker. Only when we put the two together do we realize that social justice and righteousness arise in humans who are healed and forgiven by God. We do not know yet how this will happen; Isaiah will explain this in detail in the next section (chaps. 38–55). But we cannot adequately express the prophet's teaching unless we put verses 13–16 together with verse 24 as a single communication from left and right stereo speakers.

This illustration shows that we cannot read the text in a linear manner, like we read scientific texts derived from a Greek and

Roman heritage. Only when we grasp the literary methods of ancient Hebrew writers can we properly understand the text.

How Grasping the Repetitive Patterns Can Illuminate Difficult Texts

If we grasp the character and nature of Hebrew literature, we can deal with difficult passages in the text as well as clarify the literary structure of the text as a whole. Once again the book of Isaiah helps us see how. I have argued elsewhere that the book of Isaiah as a whole comes from a single author who lived and wrote in the eighth century BC—a man named Isaiah.[3] In fact, the literary structure of the overall book demonstrates the coherence of this work.

Returning to our sound-system analogy, we can consider the Honda Acura RL. This vehicle is a full-size luxury sedan equipped with a sound system that produces DTS 5.1 surround sound, which is distributed from fourteen Bose speakers. A demo DVD explains that the music was recorded by twenty-six microphones before being distributed over eight channels. Similarly, the book of Isaiah develops its plot structure by presenting the central theme of the transformation of Zion seven times.[4] The "music" of Isaiah is like that of a DTS 5.1 surround-sound system; or, even better, Isaiah resembles the newer DTS 7.1 surround-sound system, which distributes the music over seven channels as it describes the transformation of Zion, in all seven of its major sections, like a seven-channel audio system. As outlined in chart 3.1, Isaiah details the path from a corrupt Zion in the old creation to a renewed and transformed Zion in the new creation.

---

3. Peter J. Gentry, "The Literary Macrostructures of the Book of Isaiah and Authorial Intent," in *Bind Up the Testimony: Exploration in the Genesis of the Book of Isaiah*, ed. Daniel Block and Richard L. Schultz (Peabody, MA: Hendrickson, 2015), 227–53.

4. See Barry G. Webb, "Zion in Transformation: A Literary Approach to Isaiah," in *The Bible in Three Dimensions: Essays in Celebration of Forty Years of Biblical Studies in the University of Sheffield*, ed. D. J. A. Clines, Stephen E. Fowl, and Stanley E. Porter, Journal for the Study of the Old Testament: Supplement Series 87 (Sheffield, UK: Sheffield Academic, 1990), 65–84.

Chart 3.1

The Book of Isaiah: From Zion in the Old Creation to Zion in the New

1. The Judgment and Transformation of Zion, Part 1   1:2–2:4
2. The Judgment and Transformation of Zion, Part 2   2:5–4:6
3. The Judgment of the Vineyard and the Coming King   5:1–12:6
4. The City of Man vs. the City of God   13:1–27:13
5. Trusting the Nations vs. Trusting the Word of YHWH   28:1–37:38
6. Comfort and Redemption for Zion and the World   38:1–55:13
7. The Servants of YHWH and the New Creation   56:1–66:24

In other words, we can divide the book of Isaiah into seven distinct conversations or discourses. In each one Isaiah is dealing with the topic of how we get from a corrupt Jerusalem in the first creation—a Jerusalem characterized by covenant disloyalty due to idolatry and lack of social justice—to a renewed, restored, transformed Zion in a new creation.

Chapter 1 introduces the charge of covenant disloyalty, and after Isaiah describes how the disloyalty will be dealt with by divine justice, he ends with a glorious vision of a future, renewed Zion in chapter 2:1–4, where all nations come to Zion to receive instruction from Yahweh.[5]

From 2:5 through 4:6, Isaiah details a second time the lack of social justice and the process of judgment and restoration planned by Yahweh. Again this section ends with a glorious vision of the future Zion.

The third section runs from Isaiah 5 through 12 and begins to expand on the themes a third time in the context of a complicated crisis in which tiny Judah is caught between the pincers of a threat of attack by Assyria, on the one hand, and the threat of an anti-Assyrian coalition, on the other. The crux of this crisis is the bad leadership provided by the incumbent Davidic kings Ahaz and

---

5. Although the Hebrew word *tôrâ* is normally translated "law," it really means the direction or instruction given by the Lord to his people who are in a covenant relationship with him of faithful, loyal love and trust. This word does not have the meaning of a law code as commonly understood in our Greek and Roman heritage.

Hezekiah. This section also ends with a description of a renewed Zion, focusing on a future king and a second exodus, giving us a glorious vision of the future.

In this section, chapters 5–12, a central component in the plot structure is introduced. We have a tale of two kings: Ahaz and Hezekiah. Contrary to what many scholars think, this king theme carries all the way through to the end of the book. Later, the sixth section is introduced by chapters 38 and 39, which deal with Hezekiah as an introduction to chapters 40–55, with its focus on the servant king; and the conquering/saving king is also predominant in chapters 55–66 at the center of the final section, 61:1–63:6.

While the focus in the third section is on Judah and Jerusalem, the fourth section deals with the topic of the nations and their relationship to Zion. According to the Abrahamic covenant, only by seeking refuge in Zion and its king can the people hope to escape divine judgment as well.

The fifth section ties together the previous two sections by focusing on whether people, either those in Judah or those in the nations outside, are trusting in themselves, their own military technology and political strategies, or whether they are simply trusting in Yahweh, the true king of Zion. Again, like the fourth section, which ends with a big banquet on a mountain where death is banished forever, the fifth section ends with the desert, brought about by trusting in humans, becoming a beautiful new Eden as those redeemed by Yahweh travel to it.

The sixth section, chapters 38–55, describes in detail the means and method by which God will bring deliverance to the tiny group remaining who believe and rely solely on his Word. God will use Cyrus as his servant to bring his people out of exile in Babylon and a future king, a mysterious "servant" of Yahweh who will bring Yahweh's people out of exile in terms of their relationship to him.

The last section, chapters 56–66, returns to the corruption of the present Zion and details the true servants of the Lord as they move toward a brand-new heaven and earth in chapter 65.

With this whirlwind tour of Isaiah in our minds, we can now illustrate how coming across a difficult passage can lead us to find a parallel passage in another section where the same topic is treated, and perhaps Isaiah will expand on the idea there. Or it could be that having treated a topic in great detail in an earlier section, Isaiah may make an extremely brief and condensed reference to the earlier treatment that can be understood only from the earlier section.

Examples of How Repetition Can Aid Interpretation

First, we come across a strange text in Isaiah 34:5–6:

> For my sword has drunk its fill in the heavens;
>> behold, it descends for judgment upon Edom,
>> upon the people I have devoted to destruction.
> The LORD has a sword; it is sated with blood;
>> it is gorged with fat,
>> with the blood of lambs and goats,
>> with the fat of the kidneys of rams.
> For the LORD has a sacrifice in Bozrah,
>> a great slaughter in the land of Edom. (ESV)

What on earth does the Lord mean when he says that his "sword has drunk its fill in the heavens; behold, it descends for judgment upon Edom"? There is a passage in an earlier section that explains in plain prose what is described here in metaphors and figures of speech:

> On that day the LORD will punish
>> the host of heaven, in heaven,
>> and the kings of the earth, on the earth.
> They will be gathered together
>> as prisoners in a pit;
> they will be shut up in a prison,
>> and after many days they will be punished.
>> (Isa. 24:21–22 ESV)

In the ancient world, people believed in a close connection between events on earth and events in heaven. According to the Bible, every kingdom consists of human subjects, a human ruler, and a heavenly principality or power who rules over the earthly king and kingdom. This is also clear from Daniel 7 and 10 where we see heavenly beings or princes in charge of the nations and behind the activities of the nations.

Isaiah also mentions the heavenly powers who must be punished. Just as in 24:21, where God punishes first the evil spiritual powers ruling over the nations and then the nations themselves, so in 27:1 he punishes the dark powers in heaven, "Leviathan the fleeing serpent," before his sword comes to the earth to deal with nations in rebellion against him. The language here comes from Deuteronomy 32:40–42, where the nations whom God has used to discipline his own people have wrongly concluded that they achieved the victory by their own power and the power of their false gods. So God will judge the nation of Edom as representative of all nations in rebellion against God. In Isaiah 34:5 the statement that the sword of Yahweh will drink its fill in the heavens and descend to the earth means the same thing as what we find in 24:21–22. God will first judge the heavenly rulers and then the earthly kings of the corresponding earthly kingdoms.

When Isaiah goes round his topic again—and repetition is guaranteed in Hebrew writing—we can connect parts where he is saying the same thing in slightly different ways and use the clearer expression to explain the more difficult one. Another example is found in 32:14–16:

> For the palace is forsaken,
> > the populous city deserted;
> the hill and the watchtower
> > will become dens forever,
> a joy of wild donkeys,
> > a pasture of flocks;
> until the Spirit is poured upon us from on high,

and the wilderness becomes a fruitful field,
and the fruitful field is deemed a forest.
Then justice will dwell in the wilderness,
and righteousness abide in the fruitful field. (ESV)

Isaiah is describing the coming judgment for covenant violation: exile (in Babylon; cf. Deut. 28:63–67). When the foreign nations attack, the palace will be forsaken and the populous city of Jerusalem deserted. Notice that in verse 15 "the Spirit is poured upon us from on high," and as a result the wilderness becomes a fruitful field. This is a compact statement that summarizes Isaiah 11:1–9, which can be outlined as shown in chart 3.2.

Chart 3.2

1.	Gifts Given to a Future King	11:1–3a
2.	The Rule of the Future King	11:3b–5
3.	The Harmony of the Future Kingdom	11:6–7
4.	The Victory of the Knowledge of the Lord	11:8–9

Isaiah 11:1–9 is a poem consisting of four stanzas. The first stanza speaks of a future king receiving gifts from the Spirit of God. There are seven gifts organized into three pairs plus one. In the second stanza, the king uses these gifts to get rid of evildoers and establish a kingdom characterized by the social justice found in the Mosaic covenant. Then in the third stanza a new creation comes into being where there is harmony among all people and between people and animals. Finally, in the fourth stanza, the whole earth is a holy mountain where even the most vulnerable member is no longer threatened by the Snake who brought evil in Genesis 3, and everyone knows the Lord in a relationship of faithful, loyal love and humble obedience and trust with their creator God.

What we see, then, in Isaiah 32:15 is that the entire sequence of 11:1–9 is compacted to a single statement: the Spirit comes, and a new creation results. Isaiah returns to this topic in chapter 35 and develops it further, going around the topic again. Consider 32:3–4:

> Then the eyes of those who see will not be closed,
>   and the ears of those who hear will give attention.
> The heart of the hasty will understand and know,
>   and the tongue of the stammerers will hasten to speak
>   distinctly. (ESV)

Chapter 32 is divided into six sections that develop the theme of destruction followed by deliverance. But what does it mean that "the eyes of those who see will not be closed"? This is probably a reference to Isaiah 6:10, which we have already quoted. Those hearing Isaiah's words had rejected his message. The blindness and deafness is spiritual. Isaiah 29:11 is another discourse where the same topic comes up in a different way:

> And the vision of all this has become to you like the words of a book that is sealed. When men give it to one who can read, saying, "Read this," he says, "I cannot, for it is sealed." (ESV)

A similar statement is found in 35:5–6a:

> Then the eyes of the blind shall be opened,
>   and the ears of the deaf unstopped;
> then shall the lame man leap like a deer,
>   and the tongue of the mute sing for joy. (ESV)

In context, this appears to be a prediction of the physically blind being healed. This would correlate with Isaiah 61:1 and the fulfillment of that text in Matthew 11:2–4 and Luke 7:18–23. Nonetheless, perhaps it also refers to those in a broken relationship with God who now are given spiritual sight—the ability to believe the message.

Many aspects of the text can be opened up and properly understood once we grasp the manner in which these authors of the distant past communicate. As a final example, how would we capture the hope for the future offered by Isaiah's message as a whole? Well, we would have to look to the end of each of the seven sections where he describes the renewed, transformed Zion. In 2:1–4 Mount Zion is higher than all others, and all nations come to hear instruction from Yahweh. In 4:2–6 the city is purified but is described in language similar to what the people experienced in Moses's day, when they journeyed through the desert to the Promised Land. Only now, the cloud representing the glory of Yahweh covers the whole city, not just the tabernacle or temple, which implies that the entire city is now the temple.

We have already summarized Isaiah 11, where a future king uses gifts of the Spirit to get rid of evil and establish social justice; a new creation ensues in which all know the Lord. Isaiah 25 portrays a banquet on a mountain where the shroud of death is forever removed, and chapter 35 contrasts the desert created by humans trusting in themselves to a desert turned into Eden as the new people of God journey home from exile. Isaiah 54 and 55 describe the benefits of the new covenant, not just for Israel but for all the nations. Finally, chapter 65 depicts the new heavens and the new earth, i.e., the new Jerusalem, for the two are coextensive. We need to listen to these seven speakers all at once in order to catch the idea Isaiah is communicating.

4

The Purpose of the Oracles
concerning the Foreign Nations

In this chapter we deal head-on with a fundamental question that arises in the minds of many readers of the Old Testament prophets: Why are there so many *long*, *boring* speeches concerning all kinds of countries and nations in the ancient world that are apparently entirely irrelevant to us today? Each of the three major prophets— Isaiah, Jeremiah, and Ezekiel—contains such speeches. In Isaiah these oracles cover chapters 13–27. In Jeremiah, chapters 46–51 are devoted to the foreign nations. In Ezekiel, chapters 25–32 concern non-Israelite peoples. Taken together, the space devoted to these oracles ranges somewhere between 12 and 23 percent of these books—a significant portion of the overall story. In the Book of the Twelve, also known as the Minor Prophets, a number of the books are completely focused on just one of the foreign nations: Obadiah focuses on Edom, Jonah and Nahum on Nineveh (the Assyrians), Habakkuk on the Babylonians, and Zephaniah on the Cushites (southern Egypt and Sudan), while Amos covers six foreign nations.

Importance of the Song of Moses

Like most things in the prophetic books, the oracles concerning the nations are explained by the book of Deuteronomy, particularly chapter 32, which contains the Song of Moses. At the conclusion of Deuteronomy—in fact, at the conclusion of the entire first five books we call the "Pentateuch"—Moses summarizes everything in a catchy song, although modern musicians have failed to recognize it as such. In Deuteronomy 32, Moses sums up the current history of Israel and predicts the future history of Israel right through to Revelation 22, the end of the Bible. We see in the song that the relationship of the foreign nations and their future is connected directly to the future of Israel, as we ought to expect from the covenant promises to Abraham in Genesis 12:1–3.

Given the role of this song in portraying much of redemptive history, we must try to understand how it relates to the long sections on the foreign nations in the prophets. As usual, we need to begin by observing the literary structure, since we can construct from it an overview of the whole song, and this in turn will determine our understanding of individual lines and statements. This poem is not easy to divide into sections or stanzas. The following division is based on analyzing Hebrew poetry in the manner described by M. P. O'Connor[1] and also by the linguistic science of discourse grammar, an approach that considers grammatical markers that function above the boundaries of individual clauses and sentences and operate at the larger level of the text as a whole. Yahweh and Israel are married by virtue of the covenant at Sinai. But Israel will cheat on Yahweh by serving idols and practicing social injustice. So the song is a kind of lawsuit, where Yahweh, the offended party, mixes accusations, exhortations, and oaths that promise exile and judgment on Israel, the offending party, all as clearly defined by the covenant document agreed upon by both parties (see Deuteronomy 28).

---

1. M. P. O'Connor, *Hebrew Verse Structure* (Winona Lake, IN: Eisenbrauns, 1980, 1997).

Chart 4.1

Outline of Deuteronomy 32: The Song of Moses

Stanza 1: Faithful God, Faithless People	vv. 1–6
A. Invocation of Witnesses	v. 1
B. Blessing of the Song's Teaching	v. 2
C. Theme: Describing the Character/Greatness of Yahweh	v. 3
D. Innocence of Offended Party / Guilt of Defendant (How Can Kindness Be Treated This Way?)	vv. 4–6
Stanza 2: Cross-Examination Shows Favor of Yahweh to Israel	vv. 7–14
A. Cross-Examination 1: Yahweh's Electing Love	vv. 7–19
B. Cross-Examination 2: Yahweh's Electing Love	vv. 10–14
Stanza 3: Denunciation and Judgment of Israel	vv. 15–25
A. Israel Grew Prosperous and Rebelled: Forgot God	vv. 15–18
B. Yahweh Is Angered by Israel	vv. 19–20
C. Yahweh Invokes Retributive Justice (They Provoke Him with a No-God; He Will Provoke with a No-People)	vv. 21–23
D. The Covenant Curses Are Invoked upon Israel	vv. 24–25
Stanza 4: Israel's and the Nations' Perceptions of Events	vv. 26–38
A. Complete Destruction of Israel Was Justified but Not Carried Out	vv. 26–27
B. Calamity Due to Covenant Curses, Not to Enemies' Power	vv. 28–30
C. Enemies' Worship of False Gods Leads Culture to Destruction	vv. 31–33
D. Yahweh Will Judge Enemies and Show His People Compassion (After Leaving Them to the Consequences of Their Idolatry)	vv. 34–36 / vv. 37–38
Stanza 5: The Vindication and Vengeance of Yahweh	vv. 39–43
A. Yahweh Swears to Take Vengeance on His Enemies	vv. 39–42
B. Yahweh Promises to Atone for the Land of His People	v. 43

The song opens with Moses calling the heavens and the earth as legal witnesses. The song brings a benefit to hearers as significant as rain showers that cause growth. Moses's theme is the greatness of the Name, i.e., the being and character of Yahweh.

Stanza 1.D shows that Yahweh has been faithful and kind in the covenant relationship, but Israel has not. The offended party, Yahweh, asks, how can kindness be treated this way? It is like biting the hand that feeds you.

Stanza 2 begins the cross-examination and goes back to the origins of the nations. There Israel was marked out for special love and treatment by the creator God.

The cross-examination continues in stanza 2.B, where Israel's recent history is recounted using metaphors of birds caring for their young. Finding Israel in the desert is a reference to the exodus. During the desert journey and in the land of Canaan, Yahweh provided richly for Israel's welfare.

Stanza 3 indicts Israel as in a case in court: the nation prospered and in prosperity forgot their God. There are different words in Hebrew for "to forget." One entails a mental lapse, the other a moral lapse. Here, Moses is talking about a moral problem. The matter of "forgetting God" is the subject of Moses's preaching in Deuteronomy 6–11, especially 8:11–17:

> Take care lest you forget the LORD your God by not keeping his commandments and his rules and his statutes, which I command you today, lest, when you have eaten and are full and have built good houses and live in them, and when your herds and flocks multiply and your silver and gold is multiplied and all that you have is multiplied, then your heart be lifted up, and you forget the LORD your God, who brought you out of the land of Egypt, out of the house of slavery, who led you through the great and terrifying wilderness, with its fiery serpents and scorpions and thirsty ground where there was no water, who brought you water out of the flinty rock, who fed you in the wilderness with manna that your fathers did not

know, that he might humble you and test you, to do you good
in the end. Beware lest you say in your heart, "My power and
the might of my hand have gotten me this wealth." (ESV)

Forgetting God entails arrogance. It's to look at our health, family,
job, property, and success and say, "Who needs the Lord? I am
getting on fine by myself, thank you."

In stanza 3.C Yahweh invokes retributive justice. It is the basis
for all the social justice in the entire Pentateuch or the Torah. Retributive justice means that when someone wrongs another, exact
repayment must be made. The repayment must be as much as,
no more, than the amount of damage caused or wrong done (Lev.
24:17–22).

In this particular situation, Israel has angered and provoked
Yahweh by serving no-gods, nonentities, so Yahweh will anger
and provoke Israel by no-peoples, i.e., the foreign nations. We
see God's plan concerning the foreign nations in relation to Israel
beginning to unfold.

Yahweh invokes the covenant curses upon Israel in stanza 3.D.
His actions are not the capricious wrath of a vindictive deity but
part and parcel of the agreement that Israel joyfully and will-
ingly made with Yahweh at Sinai and in the expanded and revised
form in Deuteronomy. Deuteronomy 28 spells out the blessings
for covenant loyalty and the curses for cheating on one's covenant
partner. The last part of stanza 4 is extremely significant. Yahweh
is tempted to completely erase the nation of Israel from the face
of the earth, and only one thing halts him from pursuing this
fully justified line of action: he does not want the enemy nations
believing that they can conquer Israel by their own prowess and
military power.

The final covenant curse is exile, which entails God's handing
his people over to some foreign nation and allowing them to capture the Israelites and take them into captivity. The enemy nation
will conclude for a time that they have captured Israel because

their god(s) are bigger and more powerful than Yahweh. When the Assyrians come and conquer all the cities of Judah, this is exactly what they initially said:

> Thus shall you speak to Hezekiah king of Judah: "Do not let your God in whom you trust deceive you by promising that Jerusalem will not be given into the hand of the king of Assyria. Behold, you have heard what the kings of Assyria have done to all lands, devoting them to destruction. And shall you be delivered? Have the gods of the nations delivered them, the nations that my fathers destroyed, Gozan, Haran, Rezeph, and the people of Eden who were in Telassar? Where is the king of Hamath, the king of Arpad, the king of the city of Sepharvaim, the king of Hena, or the king of Ivvah?" (Isa. 37:10–13 ESV)

Stanza 4 of Moses's song is difficult to understand, mainly because we have to carefully track the pronouns and the people to whom they refer. The foolish nation is Israel, as in verse 6. Israel does not understand that the *only* reason for their defeat by nations much more powerful is their covenant violation. It is not because the gods of the foreign nations are superior to Yahweh. Then imagery of grapevines is used to show that the fruit comes from the root. A civilization may appear to be grand and glorious, but if it is built on false gods or idols, it will not last. It is doomed to destruction. Sodom and Gomorrah produced the best grapes in the entire land,[2] yet their civilization was built on social injustice. This is the poison mentioned in verses 32–33. So stanza 4.C–D shows that Yahweh will bring destruction to the foreign nations who have built civilizations on false gods and will judge Israel for her covenant infidelity.

In the last stanza, stanza 5, Yahweh makes an oath and solemnly swears. What will he do? Based solely on his own character,

---

2. See Bryant G. Wood, "The Discovery of the Sin Cities of Sodom and Gomorrah," *Bible and Spade* 12 (1999): 66–80.

he will punish the foreign nations for idolatry, he will rescue Israel, and he will atone for his land.

Throughout all the stanzas of this song run two themes: (1) negatively, God will bring judgment upon the arrogant idolatry of the foreign nations, and (2), positively, he will fulfill the Abrahamic covenant by using Israel to bring deliverance and salvation to the rest of the world. God called Abraham and blessed him so that he might bless all the nations of the world (Acts 3:25–26).

This song and the messages in the prophets concerning the foreign nations would bring huge comfort and encouragement to the people of God. The oracles show that Yahweh controls and governs not just Israel but the entire world. He is sovereign over all nations. Only Yahweh is sovereign. He alone defines what is right and wrong, he alone makes future plans that shall certainly come to pass, and he alone acts in history. No one and no nation can challenge his right, spurn his will, or thwart his actions. What an encouragement to the Israelites as they watched the events played by superpowers on the stage of history.

Messages concerning the Foreign Nations in Isaiah 13–27

The sections concerning the foreign nations in Isaiah are found in chapters 13–27. Although many commentators and translations of the Bible speak of "oracles *against* the foreign nations," it is better to translate the preposition in Hebrew using the word "concerning," i.e., "oracles concerning the foreign nations." The reason for this is that each one of the messages not only announces future judgment for a particular nation but also indicates how it may find deliverance by seeking refuge in Zion. Thus the term "against" does not adequately represent the content of these passages.

There are fifteen oracles in Isaiah 13–27 arranged in three groups of five. Here we can briefly summarize the first five oracles to show how God plans to judge the nations for arrogant idolatry and also how he calls and invites them to find salvation through Israel and particularly through a future king of Israel. Foundational to the flow of thought here are the covenants Yahweh made with Abraham and David, since the covenant made at Sinai has been violated and is now at an end. We will briefly consider the literary structures of the first five oracles concerning the foreign nations to see how the nations' relationship to Zion becomes central to their blessing and judgment, in accordance with Genesis 12:1–3.

Oracle concerning Babylon (Isaiah 13:1–14:27)

A The Day of YHWH		13:2–16
	B Overthrow of Babylon	13:17–22
		C Restoration of YHWH's People	14:1–2
	B' Overthrow of Babylon	14:3–23
A' The End of Assyrian Power		14:24–27

As is common in Hebrew literature, this oracle concerning Babylon and Assyria (two world powers associated at that time) is divided into two larger subunits, Isaiah 13:2–22 and 14:3–27. Isaiah 14:1–2 occurs at the center of a chiastic structure that portrays Israel as restored and the nations among it as male and female servants. This second point may be construed as many of Jesus's disciples understood it.[3] They foresaw Israel on top and all nations subject to it. However, since Isaiah 14:1–2 should be interpreted in light of Isaiah 38–55 and 56–66, this is a misinterpretation. First, chapters 38–55 introduce a future servant who will do for Israel what she has failed to do herself in service to Yahweh. Second, Isaiah 54:17 clearly demonstrates that the servant will spawn *servants* as a result of his finished work. Finally, chapters 56–66 declare that these future servants will include eunuchs and foreigners who function as Levites and priests in the restored worshiping community on Mount Zion. Thus, in 14:1–2 Isaiah baits his readers by speaking of the inclusion of the Gentiles.

---

3. See Acts 1:6 and the expectations of Ps. 2:9; cf. Rev. 2:27.

Oracle concerning Philistia (Isaiah 14:28-32)

The oracle concerning Philistia also divides into two sections, each half of which is repeated, creating an overall A B A′ B′ structure. Following his pronouncement of judgment upon the Philistines, the prophet announces future safety for the wretched in Zion.

A	Future Destruction for the Philistines	14:29
B	Future Safety for the Wretched in Zion	14:30
A′	Future Destruction for the Philistines	14:31
B′	Future Safety for the Wretched in Zion	14:32

At the beginning of this oracle, the Philistines are told not to celebrate because the rod that struck them is broken. Using mixed metaphors involving plants and different kinds of snakes, the oracle warns them of a future ruler who will force them to submit. While some scholars associate this with a coming Assyrian king, others see a future descendant of Ahaz. Although the interpretation of several details is uncertain, the main points are clear. With the death of the king, whether Judean or Assyrian, the Philistines are not to think they have escaped judgment. God promises safety for those in Zion but warns of total destruction for the nations who have not sought refuge with the anointed king who rules in Zion.

Oracle concerning Moab (Isaiah 15:1-16:14)

A	The Sudden Destruction of Moab	15:1
B	The Lament of the Moabites	15:2-4
C	Grief over Moab	15:5-9
D	A Plea for Safety in Zion and Moab's Pride	16:1-6
B′	The Lament of the Moabites	16:7-8
C′	The Grief of the Lord over Moab	16:9-12
A′	The Imminent Destruction of Moab	16:13-14

All three of the topics found in Isaiah 15–16 are dealt with twice, and although the structure in which they are presented and re-presented is not a perfect chiasm, 16:1–6 is clearly central. There we find this remarkable statement:

> And a throne will be established in *kindness*,
>> and one will sit on it in *faithfulness*,
>>> in the tent of David judging
>> and seeking justice
> and swift in righteousness. (v. 5)

This short declaration promises a descendant of David whose rule will exhibit perfectly all the instructions in the covenant. The word pairs *kindness-faithfulness* and *justice-righteousness* are split, in both cases, over parallel lines that form bookends for the central statement, offering another example of the latter word pair occurring at significant points within the literary sections in which they are found.

The oracle concerning Moab is emotionally charged. Not only the nation itself but Yahweh also is grieved over the judgment of Moab. Moab is commanded to pay tribute to the commander of Israel, because only there will it find safety. Yahweh calls the people of Moab "my fugitives" (16.4) and commands Zion to allow the fugitives to stay with her, although pride unfortunately prevents them from doing so. The focus of the chiastic center of the oracles, however, is on the social justice established by the Davidic king.

Oracle concerning the Superpowers (Northern Kingdom and World) (Isaiah 17:1–18:7)

A The Superpowers of This World		17:1–3
B Judgment on the Northern Kingdom		17:4–6
C People Will Turn from Idols to Creator		17:7–8
B′ Judgment on the Northern Kingdom		17:9–11
A′ The Superpowers of This World		17:12–18:7

Like the first oracle (Isa. 13:1–14:27), the fourth (17:1–18:7) consists of two corresponding sections (AB and B´A´) that are placed on either side of a central section (C). The first section (A) focuses on destruction brought to Syria and the northern kingdom by the eastern and western superpowers of the world, Assyria and Nubia. The last section (A´) takes up the topic again and shows that this terror will be limited (by God). The second section (B) deals specifically with the judgment on the northern kingdom. The fourth section (B´) matches the second and gives the reason for this judgment. In the central section (C), metaphors from the agricultural harvest in 17:5–6 anticipate the salvation of a remnant, which is portrayed, in 17:7, not in particularistic terms but in terms of humanity in general ("man").

Oracle concerning Egypt (Isaiah 19:1–20:6)

A The Smiting of Egypt in General Terms	19:1–15
B The Healing of Egypt	19:16–25
A´ The Smiting of Egypt in Detailed Terms	20:1–6

Alec Motyer correctly observes that the oracle concerning Egypt is divided into three parts, with the healing of Egypt at the center of the chiasm.[4] The future portrayed for Egypt involves five cities, including Heliopolis, which will speak the language of Canaan. The prophet also envisions an altar to Yahweh in the midst of Egypt and a memorial pillar of stone at the border, the latter similar to the one set up by the newly established nation of Israel in the book of Joshua (22:10–11). Accordingly, in the future Egypt will become a country like Israel. The climax appears in Isaiah 19:24–25:

> In that day Israel will be the third with Egypt and Assyria, a
> blessing in the midst of the earth, whom the LORD of hosts has

---

4. J. Alec Motyer, *The Prophecy of Isaiah: An Introduction and Commentary* (Downers Grove, IL: IVP Academic, 2015), 163.

blessed, saying, "Blessed be Egypt my people, and Assyria the work of my hands, and Israel my inheritance." (ESV)

Here Isaiah predicts that the renewal and restoration of Zion will involve taking Israel's worst enemies and incorporating them into the one people of God, giving names to Assyria and Egypt that once were used only of Israel.

So read these long messages concerning the nations with great interest. God is sovereign over the world. He will hold the nations accountable for worshiping the creation instead of the Creator. The only form of deliverance and salvation is found in Israel and in her coming King. It requires faith to believe this. It is like saying to China or the United States, "A ruler is coming to Liechtenstein—you will find the resolution of all your problems in him."

5

Describing the Future, Part 1

Typology and the New Exodus

The Israelite prophet usually called his experience a "vision." Nonetheless, the expression may apply to the experience on any or all of his five senses (see Isa. 21:3). His prophetic experience gives him access to the heavenly court, where Yahweh is enthroned.

The Nature of Hebrew Prophecy

In a number of places in the Bible, we are given a glimpse of the court of heaven, where God is surrounded by angels, or the heavenly host, who are called in the earlier parts of the Old Testament "sons of God" or simply "gods." One example occurs in the book of Job. Job 1:6 states that "there was a day when the sons of God came to present themselves before the LORD, and the Adversary [the *śāṭān*] also came among them." Another example is found in Psalm 82, which begins with the words, "God has taken his place in the divine assembly; he gives judgment among the gods." In 1 Kings 22:19, when the king of Judah and the king of Israel are seeking the divine will about whether to join together in an attack upon the Arameans, we see that the prophet Micaiah has access to the assembly of the court of heaven where God announces his decisions. In verse 19 we read, "Micaiah continued, 'Therefore hear the word of the LORD: I saw the LORD sitting on his throne with all the host of heaven standing around him on his right and on his left.'" Isaiah, too, as a prophet, has access to the divine assembly, and here he announces a court case between God and the nations.[1]

So the prophet hears and sees the divine decisions that concern the governing of particular individuals, nations, or situations. The prophet does not necessarily understand all he is reporting. Yet with broad strokes the prophet paints a panoramic picture in which the near and distant futures of his vision are set side by side.

The Near and Distant Future in Isaiah 7–11

Chart 5.1 contains the sequence of visions from Isaiah 7:1–11:6. An N marks the vision as applying to the immediate or near future; an F indicates a prediction of the distant or far future. This illustrates in a simple way how predictions of far and near future are placed side by side as Isaiah's prophecy zigzags back and forth in terms of time.[2]

Chart 5.1

	III. The Immanuel Cycle 7:1–8:18	
N	A. The Threat to the Davidic House	7:1–9
	1. Conspiracy against the Davidic House	7:1–2
	2. Response of the Prophet	7:3–6
	3. The Conspiracy Will Fail	7:7–9

---

1. 1 Kings 22:13–23 and Zechariah 3 show the connection between the heavenly court and speaking for God. Indeed, the first-person plural "Who will go for *us*?" in Isa. 6:8 confirms that as a prophet Isaiah has access to the heavenly council.

2. My outline, although my own work, has been influenced by the work of Christophe Rico, *La Mère de l'Enfant-Roi—Isaïe 7, 14* (Paris: Éditions du Cerf, 2013), 138–42.

We saw earlier from Deuteronomy 18 that a prophet was affirmed when his prophecies came true. For that reason, he would place his predictions concerning the near future next to his predictions of the distant future so that when the more immediate predictions came to pass, his hearers would be encouraged or instructed by his predictions concerning the distant future. This point alone is responsible for the fact that books such as Isaiah, Daniel, and Zechariah are divided into a part dealing with contemporary issues and a part dealing with the distant future. To deny authorship of the second part to the prophet of the first part is to misunderstand the function and nature of Hebrew prophecy as well as the literary structure and unity of these works.

The manner in which the prophet speaks of the future is determined by both the purpose of the prophecy in question and the features that constrain communication in the human world. Broadly speaking, there are three ways in which descriptions of events in the future can be made: (1) literal, plain speech (no metaphors, symbols, or types), (2) apocalyptic language, which makes heavy use of metaphors and symbols, and (3) types. Each of these three ways of communicating fulfills different functions in the literary setting in which it is found. The main focus of this chapter is to deal with the notion of types and typology.

> *Typology: events, people, and places in the
> past that become a model or pattern for
> events, people, and places in the future.*

Typology

Perhaps it might be helpful to illustrate typology and then, after-ward, define it more precisely. A major type in the Bible, in both Old and New Testaments, is the exodus, when God delivered his people Israel from bondage and slavery in Egypt. Here an event in the past becomes a model or pattern to describe future deliverance and salvation for the people of God.

Let us explore the way in which the prophets in general and Isaiah in particular use the language of God's great act of deliver-ance in Israel's past to announce and describe the future deliver-ance from exile.

Especially constructive and helpful is an essay by Bernhard W. Anderson entitled "Exodus Typology in Second Isaiah."[3] Ander-son's title is based on his belief that Isaiah 40–66 are chapters written after the time of the eighth-century prophet known as Isa-iah. Here his presuppositions lead him astray, for exodus typology is found equally in Isaiah 1–39. Anderson's interpretation better suits an approach that takes the book as a unity written by Isaiah than an approach that does not.

Anderson identifies four separate stages to the event of the exodus. Language alluding to each of these four stages is employed by Isaiah to describe the future deliverance and rescue of Israel. These four stages are as follows:[4]

---

3. Bernhard W. Anderson, "Exodus Typology in Second Isaiah," in *Israel's Prophetic Heritage: Essays in Honor of James Muilenburg*, ed. Bernhard W. Anderson and Walter Harrelson (New York: Harper, 1962), 177–95. I draw heavily upon the work of Ander-son here.

4. Ibid., 182–84.

1. The Promises to the Fathers
2. The Deliverance from Egypt
3. The Journey through the Wilderness
4. The Reentry into the Promised Land

We will briefly describe the basis in the Pentateuch or the Torah for each of these four stages and then illustrate from the book of Isaiah how the prophet employs the imagery and language of that particular stage to describe the future salvation.

First, the promises to the fathers. Here the term *fathers* refers to Abraham, Isaac, and Jacob—the nation's forefathers and patriarchs. The exodus was predicted four hundred years prior to the event, when God made a covenant with Abraham in Genesis 15:12–16:

> As the sun was going down, a deep sleep fell on Abram. And behold, dreadful and great darkness fell upon him. Then the LORD said to Abram, "Know for certain that your offspring will be sojourners in a land that is not theirs and will be servants there, and they will be afflicted for four hundred years. But I will bring judgment on the nation that they serve, and afterward they shall come out with great possessions. As for you, you shall go to your fathers in peace; you shall be buried in a good old age. And they shall come back here in the fourth generation, for the iniquity of the Amorites is not yet complete." (ESV)

In Genesis 12, 15 and 17, and 22 God promises descendants and land to the fathers. These promises are repeated in Isaiah, but this time with reference to the return of the exiles from Babylon:

> Surely your waste and your desolate places
>   and your devastated land—
> surely now you will be too narrow for your inhabitants,
>   and those who swallowed you up will be far away.
> The children of your bereavement

will yet say in your ears:
"The place is too narrow for me;
    make room for me to dwell in."
Then you will say in your heart:
    "Who has borne me these?
I was bereaved and barren,
    exiled and put away,
    but who has brought up these?
Behold, I was left alone;
    from where have these come?" (Isa. 49:19–21 ESV)

"Sing, O barren one, who did not bear;
    break forth into singing and cry aloud,
    you who have not been in labor!
For the children of the desolate one will be more
    than the children of her who is married," says
        the LORD.
"Enlarge the place of your tent,
    and let the curtains of your habitations be stretched out;
do not hold back; lengthen your cords
    and strengthen your stakes.
For you will spread abroad to the right and to the left,
    and your offspring will possess the nations
    and will people the desolate cities." (Isa. 54:1–3 ESV)

When the exiles return from Babylon, they will have family members they don't recognize, and they will have more land, because the Gentiles, the nations, will be included in the tent of Abraham. So Isaiah employs language from the promises to the ancestors of Israel and applies them to the coming salvation. There is a difference, however: the new exodus will be bigger and better. It will involve more land and seed than just ethnic Israel.

The second stage of the exodus event is the deliverance from Egypt, which involved the plagues upon the gods of Egypt, the exit from Egypt, and the crossing of the Red Sea. Language from this part of the exodus is also used by Isaiah to describe the coming rescue of Israel from exile in Babylon and exile in a broken relationship with Yahweh, i.e., slavery to sin. This second stage can be illustrated in many ways.

A key phrase of the exodus is that Yahweh delivered his people with a mighty hand and an outstretched arm (Deut. 4:34). The "arm" is applied by Isaiah to the coming salvation especially (Isa. 40:10; 48:14; 51:5, 9; 52:12; 53:1). During the exodus, by means of a pillar of cloud by day and fire by night, Yahweh went before his people and was also a "rear guard." We see these terms applied to the coming salvation in Isaiah 4:5 and 52:12. In the Song at the Sea celebrating the exodus, in Exodus 15, Yahweh is called a "man of war" (v. 3). The only other place where this phrase is applied to Yahweh is Isaiah 42:13 concerning the new exodus. In fact, Isaiah speaks of a new song in 42:10. What is the new song? To answer this question we must know what the old song is. The old song is Exodus 15, and the new song celebrates the victory of the king in the new exodus. This idea goes right through to Revelation 5:9.

The third stage of the exodus is the journey through the desert, which should have taken just days but took forty years (Deut. 1:2). In the exodus, Yahweh led his people and showed them the way (Ex. 13:21). In the coming deliverance, a call is given to prepare the way of the Lord in the desert (Isa. 40:3–5). Mark 1:1–3 identifies John (the Baptist) and Jesus as beginning to fulfill this part of the new exodus.

During the desert journey, God provided food (bread rained from the skies every day) and water (e.g., from the rock, Ex. 17:2–7; Num. 20:8). This imagery is also applied to the future salvation in Isaiah 41:17–20; 43:19–21; 48:21; and 49:10. As a matter of fact, the desert will eventually be transformed into a new Eden (Isa. 35:6–7; 49:9–11; 55:13).

The fourth and final stage of the exodus is the entrance into the Promised Land described in the book of Joshua. Note Isaiah 49:8–11:

Thus says the LORD:
"In a time of favor I have answered you;
>in a day of salvation I have helped you;
I will keep you and give you
>as a covenant to the people,
to establish the land,
>to apportion the desolate heritages,
saying to the prisoners, 'Come out,'
>to those who are in darkness, 'Appear.'
They shall feed along the ways;
>on all bare heights shall be their pasture;
they shall not hunger or thirst,
>neither scorching wind nor sun shall strike them,
for he who has pity on them will lead them,
>and by springs of water will guide them.
And I will make all my mountains a road,
>and my highways shall be raised up. (ESV)

This section is full of images from the exodus. Note in particular the end of verse 8: "to apportion the desolate heritages." This is a direct allusion to Joshua 15–19, the section describing Joshua apportioning the land of Canaan to the tribes according to their clans. Paul uses precisely this language in Colossians 1:12 to speak of the work of Jesus Christ in bringing about the new exodus.

Anderson lists a number of the passages in Isaiah where the coming rescue from exile (in Babylon and in sin) uses the language of God's great redemption in the past:[5]

Chart 5.2

Passages in Isaiah Where New Exodus Is the Theme

1.	40:3–5	The Highway in the Wilderness
2.	41:17–20	The Transformation of the Wilderness
3.	42:14–16	Yahweh Leads His People in a Way Unknown

5. Ibid., 182–83.

Passages in Isaiah Where New Exodus Is the Theme

4.	43:1–3	Passing through the Waters and the Fire
5.	43:14–21	A Way in the Wilderness
6.	48:20–21	The Exodus from Babylon
7.	49:8–12	The New Entry into the Promised Land
8.	51:9–10	The New Victory at the Sea
9.	52:11–12	The New Exodus
10.	55:12–13	Israel Shall Go Out in Joy and Peace

Ezekiel and Jeremiah as well as the other prophets continue to use images and language from the exodus to describe the coming king and his victory that brings not only physical release from Babylon but spiritual rescue from slavery to sin and incorrigible covenant violation.

But there is more to just using the exodus as a model or pattern of future salvation. The antitype to which the type points, or the reality of which the model or pattern is only a shadow, or which it foreshadows, is always bigger and greater than the type. We shall briefly consider three examples.

> Depart, depart, go out from there;
> > touch no unclean thing;
> go out from the midst of her; purify yourselves,
> > you who bear the vessels of the LORD.
> For you shall not go out in haste,
> > and you shall not go in flight,
> for the LORD will go before you,
> > and the God of Israel will be your rear guard.
> > > (Isa. 52:11–12 ESV)

This is another section where Yahweh describes bringing the exiles home using the language of the exit from Egypt. Notice that verse 12 says, "you shall not go out in haste." The Hebrew word used for "haste" (*ḥippāzōn*) occurs only three times in the entire Old Testament: Exodus 12:11, Deuteronomy 16:3, and Isaiah 52:12.

The occurrences in Exodus and Deuteronomy describe the exodus from Egypt—they went out in a hurry. They didn't have time to plan for the journey or pack properly. They just grabbed their stuff and took off.

In the new exodus, however, they will not go out in haste. They will be given time to slowly saunter out. This was true of the physical release from Babylon. There were a couple of groups that departed at different times. It is also true of the new exodus brought about by Jesus Christ. The period between his first coming and his second coming constitutes the time for bringing the exiles home, and the generosity and kindness of God are displayed in providing lots of time for his people to return to him.

The claim that the period between Jesus's first and second coming is the return from exile (i.e., slavery to sin and broken covenant relationship with God) requires proof. Note first Jeremiah 16:14–16:

> Therefore, behold, the days are coming, declares the LORD, when it shall no longer be said, "As the LORD lives who brought up the people of Israel out of the land of Egypt," but "As the LORD lives who brought up the people of Israel out of the north country and out of all the countries where he had driven them." For I will bring them back to their own land that I gave to their fathers. Behold, I am sending for many fishers, declares the LORD, and they shall catch them. And afterward I will send for many hunters, and they shall hunt them from every mountain and every hill, and out of the clefts of the rocks. (ESV)

In verses 14–16 Jeremiah describes the return from Babylon (i.e., "the north country") in plain speech. There are no figures of speech or metaphors in these verses. He does compare this deliverance to the exodus, and he does say the event will be much bigger and better than the exodus. God's people will swear not by the God of the exodus but by the one who brought about the new exodus. Then in verse 16 Jeremiah describes bringing the exiles home in terms of hunting and fishing. He will send out fishermen to bring the exiles home. So in Luke 5:10, when Jesus calls his followers and says he will make them fishers of men, it is a direct reference to Jeremiah 16. Jesus is saying metaphorically, "I have come to bring the exiles home. And I am sending you men to begin this job."

Another important passage is Isaiah 27:12–13:

> In that day from the river Euphrates to the Brook of Egypt the LORD will thresh out the grain, and you will be gleaned one by one, O people of Israel. And in that day a great trumpet will be blown, and those who were lost in the land of Assyria and those who were driven out to the land of Egypt will come and worship the LORD on the holy mountain at Jerusalem. (ESV)

This is another passage that describes bringing the exiles home, which here is compared to a harvest. The event is announced by the blowing of a trumpet—a signal in the Old Testament that usually announces the coming of a new king to rule. So in 1 Thessalonians 4, when Paul says that the return of Jesus Christ will be announced by the blowing of the trumpet of God, he is referring directly to Isaiah 27 and telling his readers that this signal that announces the coming of the king is also part of bringing the exiles home. Thus we learn that the period between Jesus's first and second comings is the time for the exiles to come home.

Another passage is Isaiah 2:2–4:

> It shall come to pass in the latter days
>   that the mountain of the house of the LORD
> shall be established as the highest of the mountains,
>   and shall be lifted up above the hills;
> and all the nations shall flow to it,
>   and many peoples shall come, and say:
> "Come, let us go up to the mountain of the LORD,
>   to the house of the God of Jacob,
> that he may teach us his ways
>   and that we may walk in his paths."

For out of Zion shall go forth the law,
    and the word of the LORD from Jerusalem.
He shall judge between the nations,
    and shall decide disputes for many peoples;
and they shall beat their swords into plowshares,
    and their spears into pruning hooks;
nation shall not lift up sword against nation,
    neither shall they learn war anymore. (ESV)

In this section Isaiah sees in a vision a picture of the future Zion. He sees it as a mountain higher than any other. In verse 3, all nations are coming to this mountain to receive instruction (*torah*) from the Lord. This image is based on the exodus when Israel came to Mount Sinai and God gave the Torah to Israel. Only here in Isaiah 2, (and in Mic. 4:1–3), Zion has replaced Sinai, and all the nations are coming to Zion to receive *torah*. This implies a new covenant that includes the nations, since the word *torah* always refers to the instruction or stipulations given in a covenant relationship. So here is another case where the new exodus has a much greater scope than the original one.

Isaiah 4 also presents a vision of the future, renewed, and transformed Zion:

In that day the growth from Yahweh will be beautiful and glorious, and the fruit of the land shall be the pride and honor of the survivors of Israel. And he who is left in Zion and survives in Jerusalem will be called holy, everyone who has been recorded for life in Jerusalem, when the Lord shall have washed away the filth of the daughters of Zion and cleansed the bloodstains of Jerusalem from its midst by a spirit of judgment and by a spirit of burning. Then the LORD will create over the whole site of Mount Zion and over her assemblies a cloud by day and smoke and the shining of a flaming fire by night; for (the) glory will be a canopy over all. There will be a booth for shade by day from the heat, and for a refuge and a shelter from the storm and rain. (vv. 2–6)

Clearly the mention of a cloud of smoke by day and a pillar of fire by night reminds the reader of the journey through the wilderness. When the tent of worship, or tabernacle, was constructed, the bright cloud that represented the glory of Yahweh settled on it. Here, however, the cloud by day and pillar by night is over *all* of the city, and the glory is a canopy over *all of Zion*. This is telling us that the entire city is a temple or place of worship. God's glory and presence are everywhere. So the new exodus is much grander than the original one.

One final illustration is necessary to demonstrate the interpretive principle under discussion, and that is Isaiah 11:11–16:

> In that day the Lord will extend his hand yet a second time to recover the remnant that remains of his people, from Assyria, from Egypt, from Pathros, from Cush, from Elam, from Shinar, from Hamath, and from the coastlands of the sea.
>
> He will raise a signal for the nations
>   and will assemble the banished of Israel,
> and gather the dispersed of Judah
>   from the four corners of the earth.
> The jealousy of Ephraim shall depart,
>   and those who harass Judah shall be cut off;
> Ephraim shall not be jealous of Judah,
>   and Judah shall not harass Ephraim.
> But they shall swoop down on the shoulder of the
>   Philistines in the west,
>   and together they shall plunder the people of the east.
> They shall put out their hand against Edom and Moab,
>   and the Ammonites shall obey them.
> And the LORD will utterly destroy
>   the tongue of the Sea of Egypt,
> and will wave his hand over the River
>   with his scorching breath,
> and strike it into seven channels,
>   and he will lead people across in sandals.

And there will be a highway from Assyria
 for the remnant that remains of his people,
as there was for Israel
 when they came up from the land of Egypt. (ESV)

According to verse 11, this section is describing Yahweh bringing the exiles or the remnant of his people home. Note the fact that it begins with the words "the Lord will extend his hand yet a second time." The phrase "extend his hand" immediately reminds us of the exodus, and the phrase "a second time" tells us that Isaiah is speaking of a future salvation as a new or *second* exodus. In verse 15 we see that Yahweh will destroy the tongue of the sea of Egypt and wave his hand over the river, i.e., the Euphrates. The Euphrates will be struck into seven channels and the people will cross in sandals.

I want to ask a question bluntly: Is Isaiah describing the event literally? Will the Red Sea be dried up and the Euphrates divided into seven channels? This did not happen for Ezra and Nehemiah in the physical return from Babylon. No, according to the interpretive principle of using images and the language of God's deliverance in the past to describe a coming salvation, we form in our minds only the idea that no obstacles will stand in God's way when he gathers the remnant of his people. This is what the rules of Hebrew literature *require* at this point. It is not a matter of defending a literal hermeneutic. It is a matter of discerning the method of communication used by the prophets and using that method to discern their intended meaning. The literal meaning is the meaning as *determined by the rules of the particular genre or kind of literature.*

The Basis for the Exodus as a Type

To deepen our understanding, we need to ask the question, Why did the biblical prophets employ the event of the exodus as a type of future salvation? To answer we need to briefly look at

Exodus 15, the Song at the Sea. This is the song sung by Moses and the people to celebrate deliverance from the army of Egyptians chasing them (Ex. 15:1). Apparently Miriam, the sister of Moses, who is called a prophetess, led the people in singing this song (vv. 20–21).

The poem or song in Exodus 15:1–18 is divided into four stanzas and arranged for antiphonal singing, a type of singing that probably requires a brief explanation. Many ancient churches or cathedrals in England and Europe are built in the shape of a cross, as in diagram 5.1.

Diagram 5.1

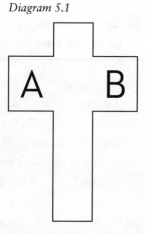

The altar and the screen are at the top of the cross; the people sit in the area below the crossbar. The letters A and B represent the area where the choir sits. The choir is divided into two halves. In some singing, parts A and B are sung together. It is also possible for the A half to sing a line or two and then for the B part to answer with a line or two. The two halves of the choir are singing to each other. This is called "antiphonal singing."

Norbert Lohfink has shown (chart 5.3) that the four stanzas of the song in Exodus 15 constitute antiphonal singing.[6]

Chart 5.3

Literary Structure of Exodus 15

A.	Praising Choir	vv. 1–7
B.	Narrative Choir	vv. 8–10
C.	Praising Choir	v. 11
D.	Narrative Choir	vv. 12–17

---

6. I am depending heavily here upon the essay by Norbert Lohfink, "The Song of Victory at the Red Sea," in Norbert Lohfink, *The Christian Meaning of the Old Testament*, trans. of *Siegeslied am Schilfmeer* by R. A. Wilson (Milwaukee: Bruce, 1968), 67–86.

The choir is divided in half (see Nehemiah 12 for an example of this kind of singing). One half is focused on praise; the other half is focused on telling the story. With this structure in mind, let us focus on the second and fourth stanzas, which relate the story of the exodus. First, consider stanza 2:

> At the blast of your nostrils the waters piled up;
>> the floods stood up in a heap;
>> the deeps congealed in the heart of the sea.
> The enemy said, "I will pursue, I will overtake,
>> I will divide the spoil, my desire shall have its fill
>>> of them.
>> I will draw my sword; my hand shall destroy them."
> You blew with your wind; the sea covered them;
>> they sank like lead in the mighty waters. (vv. 8–10 ESV)

Note the structure of these verses in chart 5.4.

Chart 5.4

B.	Narrative Choir	vv. 8–10
v. 8	Breath of Yahweh—Sea	
v. 9	Enemies Pursued	
v. 10	Breath of Yahweh—Sea	

The agent of all actions or verbs in verses 8 and 10 is Yahweh. In between verses 8 and 10 we have verse 9, where the agent of all actions or verbs is the enemy pursuing Israel. The repeated "I will" clearly emphasizes this.

The literary and poetic structure actually gives us a picture of the event. Verses 8 and 10 are like the wall of water on the left and on the right. Verse 9 is the enemy in the middle as they pursue Israel. The watery walls close in on them, and they drown. "They sank like lead in the mighty waters."

Now let us consider the fourth stanza sung also by the narrative choir in verses 12–17:

You stretched out your right hand;
  the earth swallowed them.
You have led in your steadfast love the people whom you
      have redeemed;
    you have guided them by your strength to your holy
        abode.
The peoples have heard; they tremble;
    pangs have seized the inhabitants of Philistia.
Now are the chiefs of Edom dismayed;
    trembling seizes the leaders of Moab;
    all the inhabitants of Canaan have melted away.
Terror and dread fall upon them;
    because of the greatness of your arm, they are still as
        a stone,
till your people, O LORD, pass by,
    till the people pass by whom you have purchased.
You will bring them in and plant them on your own
        mountain,
    the place, O LORD, which you have made for your
        abode,
    the sanctuary, O Lord, which your hands have
        established. (ESV)

The literary and poetic structure of the fourth stanza is the same
as that for the second, as shown in chart 5.5.

Chart 5.5

D.	Narrative Choir	vv. 12–17
vv. 12–13	Yahweh Leads into New Eden	
vv. 14–16	Avenue of Sphinxes	
v. 17	Yahweh Leads into New Eden	

This fourth stanza of the narrative choir tells of the journey
through the desert to Canaan. Israel must pass between nations
hostile to them. Instead of Israel dreading these enemies, Yahweh

places a great dread upon the enemies so that they are as still and silent as sphinxes, afraid of the Israelites. In the first and third strophes of the stanza (using the word *strophe* as a subsection of a stanza), Yahweh is the agent, and he is leading his people to a new Eden. Notice in verse 17 how Canaan is described as a mountain sanctuary, the home of Yahweh. This language comes from the garden of Eden, which was on a mountain (see Ezekiel 28). In the strophe between these two is the "Avenue of the Sphinxes," as Norbert Lohfink calls it. Israel ought to be in dread of these monster enemies, but they are silent—gripped by dread and fear placed upon them by Yahweh.

Once again, note the A B A′ pattern. Yahweh is the agent on either side, just like the wall of water in the exodus, with the enemy in the middle destroyed by dread. The main point is this: Exodus 15 was a song sung at the Red Sea, but verses 12–17 describe a future salvation. Deliverance from the enemy nations as God's people pass by them on the journey through the desert *is still future at this point in time*. Yet the wall of water on the left and on the right is a picture of how God will save them. In other words, the exodus is a model or pattern of future salvation from the very beginning. The first time they sang this song, they were using the crossing of the Red Sea as a model or pattern of how God would bring them successfully through the desert to Canaan.

Since Isaiah and the prophets understood Exodus 15 in this way, they realized that the exodus was intended to be used as a model or pattern or type of future salvation.

Principles of Typology

We are now in a position to lay out the principles of typology and the factors that determine correct interpretation: what is a type and what is not a type.[7]

---

7. Stephen J. Wellum devotes chap. 3 of Peter J. Gentry and Stephen J. Wellum, *Kingdom through Covenant: A Biblical-Theological Understanding of the Covenants*

In brief, typology is governed by four factors.

The first is correspondence between events, people, places, etc., of one time, and events, people, places, etc., of a later time. This correspondence is due to the fact that God in his providence sovereignly controls history, and he is consistent in his character so that there are repetitive patterns to his works in history.

Second is escalation from type to antitype so that the later event, person, or thing that can be said to be the fulfillment of the type is much better and greater than that which foreshadows it.

Third is biblical warrant. For something to be considered a type, there must be exegetical evidence in the original text that indicates that what the text is dealing with is intended to be a model or pattern for something to follow in history. As we just considered, deliverance through the Red Sea was intended from the start to be a model for future salvation. Thus, when the major prophets predict a future salvation through the work of a coming king, they are right to speak of it as a new exodus and describe the coming salvation in the language of God's great deliverance in the past. They are right, because they have correctly understood Exodus 15.

The fourth factor is that the progression of the covenants throughout the narrative plot structure of the Bible creates, controls, and develops the typological structures across the canon of Scripture. For example, in the covenant with creation, Adam is portrayed as a king-priest who must be an obedient son in relation to God and a servant king in relation to creation. This role is taken up by Noah in the covenant with God that reaffirms the covenant with creation. Next, in the covenant with Abraham the king-priest role devolves upon him.[8] In Exodus 19, we see how Israel as a nation is called to be an obedient son and servant

---

(Wheaton, IL: Crossway, 2012), to a discussion of typology. See also Peter J. Gentry, "The Significance of Covenants in Biblical Theology," *Southern Baptist Journal of Theology* 20/1 (2016): 9–33.

8. See Peter J. Gentry and Stephen J. Wellum, *God's Kingdom through God's Covenants* (Wheaton, IL: Crossway, 2015).

king, functioning in a priestly role in relation to the nations of the world. In the Davidic covenant, this role is narrowed from the nation as a whole to the king in particular. Finally, in the new covenant, Jesus the Messiah fulfills these roles adequately and fully.[9]

---

9. This last point is based on Gentry and Wellum, *Kingdom through Covenant*, where it is argued that the succession of covenants in Scripture (creation, Noah, Abraham, Israel, David, new covenant) is the key to the plot structure of the Bible, and therefore typology, in terms of events, persons, and places foreshadowed, can all be tied to the covenants because these are the Bible's own categories for structuring its message.

6

Describing the Future, Part 2

Apocalyptic Language

One way to describe the future is to employ models or patterns from the past. Another way to describe events that may be part of a reality different from that of the hearers or readers is to use metaphors and symbolic language. That is the topic of this chapter. What are the features of Hebrew literature or the literature of the prophets that help us understand their communicative method?

What Future Is Being Described?

Imagine a prophetic voice today addressing the historical, political, and religious context in North America. He might make predictions about what will happen in six months or a year, he might predict events to happen in twenty years, or he might, rarely, announce a matter to happen in the distant future. Let us consider how these three options might be communicated to today's public.

First, in announcing events to happen next month or in six months, the cities, provinces, states, countries, and country leaders in his prophecy would likely be the same as today. He could describe in plain speech without metaphors or symbolic language the events about to happen. He could name an individual or a city or a place known to all and describe in precise terms the details of the events.

Second, if he were to describe events that were to happen in twenty or two hundred years, he could theoretically take the same approach, but his hearers would not be able to grasp the implications in quite the same way. As I look back over the space of time since my childhood school days, so many things have changed. No leaders alive then are alive now. The map of the world has changed. Some countries no longer exist; new countries have sprung up in place of them. Some countries have different names. Borders have shifted. Cultures and languages and peoples have changed. Some animals and birds and insects are now extinct. How is one to describe a significant future event? If we remember that one of the key themes in the Bible is the relationship between God and his creatures, particularly humans, a prophet would use metaphors, symbolic language, and typology to speak of future events in order to keep the focus on relationships in view. Nonetheless, the biblical story is firmly rooted in space and time and the future involves specific people and places.

Third, let us consider how a prophet would announce something to happen two to six thousand years into the future. The plan and program to renew and restore a broken world require time; real solutions are rarely instant. Consider, for example, the prophecy in Genesis 3:15, which was fulfilled two thousand years later. How would a prophet communicate effectively about this future scenario? By way of illustrating the answer, imagine a person from the Western world traveling deep into the jungles of Papua New Guinea in the year 2000. He has linguistic training and is able to decipher the language from the native speaker, and he becomes friends with the native people. One day, a person from the tribe sees the linguist typing on his Apple Macintosh computer.

"What are you doing?" she asks. "And how does this thing work?"

Well, there would be no point in giving her a literal description of electricity and bits and bytes and binary math. The only way to communicate would be through metaphors and symbols. And the communication could be extremely effective just at that level alone. Literal details about computing would be unnecessary.

Illustration from Isaiah 13–27

Let us look at the messages in Isaiah 13–27 concerning the foreign nations to see that they operate on exactly these three levels.[1]

Chart 6.1

Overview of Isaiah 13–27

A	B	C
Babylon (13:1–14:27)	The Desert by the Sea (21:1–10)	The City of Wasteland (24:21–23)
Philistia (14:28–32)	Silence (Dumah) (21:11–12)	Zion's King (24:21–23)
Moab (15:1–16:14)	Evening (Arabia) (21:13–17)	The Great Banquet (25:1–12)
Damascus/Ephraim (17:1–18:7)	The Valley of Vision (22:1–25)	The City of God (26:1–20)
Egypt (19:1–20:6)	Tyre (23:1–18)	The Final Gathering (27:1–13)

Fifteen prophetic messages concerning the foreign nations are arranged in three groups of five. Note that the fourth message in each group of five deals specifically with the people of God in some way. The arrangement is not haphazard.

While most of these messages are written in poetry, the first ten have prose headings or titles. These titles generally orient the reader to the geographical or ethnic group that is addressed by the

---

1. Chart 6.1 adapted from J. Alec Motyer, *The Prophecy of Isaiah: An Introduction and Commentary* (Downers Grove, IL: IVP Academic, 1993), 133. Used with permission.

prophet. The geographical locations for the first five messages are simple and straightforward. Every person in Israel knows these countries. Babylon is in the far east, Philistia is in the near west, Moab in the near east, Ephraim and Damascus are to the north, and Egypt is in the far west and south. The messages cover the countries around Israel systematically.

The second set of five messages begins in Isaiah 21. While these messages also have prose headings, the titles are mysterious. For example, in 21:1 we have "The oracle concerning the wilderness of the sea." Where on earth is that? The reader knows all the places mentioned in the first set of five oracles, but this particular place wasn't part of twelfth-grade Israelite geography. So the reader must continue reading. Only toward the end (21:9) does he discover that the author is describing Babylon. After divine judgment brings complete destruction, Babylon will be a desolate spot on the Persian Gulf—indeed a desert by the sea, inhabited by various types of owls (see 13:21–22).

In Isaiah 21:11–12 we have an oracle concerning "Dumah," another location beyond twelfth-grade geography in Israel. Could the author be referring to Dumah, Dedan, and Tema, oases in the North Arabian trade routes? According to Isaiah 39 King Hezekiah of Judah was expecting help from the Babylonians against the Assyrians. One secret way to get from Babylon to Judah was to cross the desert using these oases. In Isaiah 21:11b Seir is mentioned, which seems to refer to Edom. A watchman is waiting for a message during the night. Would help come to Judah via Edom during the night? The word *Dumah* can mean "silence." Perhaps it is a play on words concerning Edom. The devastation in the country from which help is expected is so great that there is nothing but silence—no help is coming after all!

In 21:13–15 there is an oracle concerning Arabia. Does the word refer to Arabia or is it a noun meaning "desert" or perhaps a play on the word for "evening"? There is uncertainty in translating this word. It appears to deal with fugitives and refugees coming from these oases in the North Arabian desert. Apparently Babylon has fallen, and no help is coming from there at all. The sun has set on Babylon, so evening comes without help.

Then in Isaiah 22 we have an oracle concerning the valley of vision. We have never heard of this place either. As we continue to read, we discover that Isaiah is speaking of the city of Jerusalem and the plans Yahweh has for it. Only the last message, in Isaiah 23, mentions a place well known: Tyre.

Whether the interpretations I suggest are all correct is immaterial. The main point is that in the second set of five messages, Isaiah is playing games with words. The messages are more like parables—only those in the remnant with ears to hear and eyes to see and hearts to understand will be able to grasp the comfort from these messages (see Isa. 6:9–10). Some of the events may be further away in time than the events foretold in the first five.

When the reader comes to the third set of five messages, there are no prose headings. No geographical places are mentioned. The language seems to speak about the whole world in a general way. Here Isaiah seems to be dealing with a distant future. His language is full of metaphors and symbols, so much so that scholars have labeled chapters 24–27 Isaiah's "Little Apocalypse." It is time, then, to ask, what does this word *apocalypse* or the adjective *apocalyptic* really mean? The answer may be quite different from what we are given in the movies from Hollywood.

Apocalyptic

Definition

No doubt you have discovered from reading books such as Daniel or Zechariah that these do not fit the normal pattern for prophets. True, Zechariah begins in an ordinary sort of way, with a call to repentance, and Daniel commences with stories of courageous Jews who excelled in faithfulness during years of exile and oppression by foreign overlords. Then we enter a strange world of visions. Daniel has visions containing weird beasts coming up out of the sea, and

Zechariah sees a gigantic flying scroll, ten feet by thirty feet—no doubt the divine word in a special edition for the spiritually blind. If we are going to make any headway in this strange world, the first thing we must do is come to grips with the genre or kind of literature we are reading. What sort of literature is this? How do the authors of this stuff communicate, assuming they intend to make some sense at all? At least part of these books appears in a genre called "apocalyptic," so I will begin with a description of apocalyptic and the approach necessary to properly understand this literary world.

While it is difficult to define *apocalyptic*, a consensus has emerged that the word refers to a kind of literature, not to a community or an approach to theology.

The word *apocalyptic* comes from the Greek title of the book of Revelation in the New Testament. Moreover, the first verse of Revelation directly alludes to Daniel 2 (vv. 28–30, 45) where we discover that God is the one who reveals secrets.[2] Apocalyptic has to do with revealing secrets, usually about the future.

Apocalyptic literature in the Bible and in the period of Second Temple Judaism, from 250 BC to AD 250, has a number of common characteristics and features. These can be described both briefly and simply as follows:[3]

> *Narrative framework.* Apocalyptic normally has a narrative framework. This means that the contents, no matter how weird, are given in the form and framework of a story.

> *Schematization of history.* Frequently, the narrative provides a schematization of history. In other words, the course of human history is arranged into periods.

> *Given by heavenly messenger.* The revelation is mediated by an angel or heavenly messenger to a human recipient, usually a

---

2. G. K. Beale, *The Book of Revelation*, New International Greek Testament Commentary (Grand Rapids, MI: Eerdmans, 1999), 50.

3. *Semeia* 14 (1979), entitled "Apocalypse: the Morphology of a Genre," was devoted entirely to this topic. This is the basis for the categories described here.

prophet or seer. We see this in Daniel, Zechariah, and Revelation. In Revelation, John wants to bow down and worship the heavenly messenger but is strictly warned not to do so.

God's-eye view of history. Since apocalyptic involves God revealing secrets, it provides a God's-eye view of human history. We will see this in particular when we compare Daniel 2 and 7. In fact, all of prophecy presents issues from God's point of view. The book of Amos opens with the words:

> The LORD roars from Zion
> > and utters his voice from Jerusalem;
> the pastures of the shepherds mourn,
> > and the top of Carmel withers. (Amos 1:2 ESV)

During the time of Amos, the people experienced great prosperity and success. It was the best of times. Yahweh didn't think so. He thought it was the worst of times. The word "roars" implies a comparison between the Lord and a lion. The lion's home is Zion or Jerusalem. His roar is so powerful that the grass on Mount Carmel sixty miles away withers. Things may be going well from the people's point of view, but God has a different perspective. The land is filled with idolatry and social injustice.

Colorful metaphors and symbols. With this focus on the divine perspective and viewpoint—the way God sees things—it is not surprising that colorful imagery and metaphors are used. By way of illustration, imagine explaining to a person from a Stone Age culture what a computer is and how electricity works. Apocalyptic includes many different kinds of symbolism. Almost all numbers in apocalyptic are symbolic.

Future hope in present trouble. The revelation almost always has to do with future deliverance and salvation. It is given in crisis, in difficult times, normally when the people of God are called to endure a period of suffering. The apocalypse

announces future rescue of the people of God and seeks to
interpret present circumstances from God's point of view and
to comfort and encourage his people to appropriate behavior
as they await final rescue. This definition applies to many
Jewish writings written mainly from 250 BC to AD 250 and
includes *1 Enoch, 4 Ezra, 2 Baruch, Apocalypse of Abraham, 3 Baruch, 2 Enoch, Testament of Levi* 2–5, the frag-
mentary *Apocalypse of Zephaniah* (not the biblical book),
and in part also to *Jubilees* and the *Testament of Abraham*,
which are heavily influenced by the biblical books of Daniel
and Zechariah.

Apocalyptic is easier to describe than to define.[4] Let me describe the hope of Israel and show the way in which this hope
was expressed.

Israel's Hope during the Second Temple Period

What kind of hope did Jewish people have after the exile, when
they had returned and rebuilt the temple? The basis of the faith
of Israel was that there is one creator God and that Israel is his
covenant people. Although Israel had returned to the land after
the exile, she was still suffering under the oppression of foreign
overlords. In a very real sense she was still in a state of exile, and
this had to be put right. Sooner or later this creator God, in covenant with Israel, must step in and honor his covenant promises.
The symbols of the covenant will be restored because the covenant will be renewed: the temple will be rebuilt, the land will be
cleansed, and the Torah will be kept perfectly by a new-covenant
people with renewed hearts. Jewish writers adapted a literary form
and a specific type of language for expressing this hope, namely
apocalyptic.

---

4. I depend here on the work of N. T. Wright, as his presentation of apocalyptic is useful.
See N. T. Wright, *The New Testament and the People of God*, vol. 1, Christian Origins and
the Question of God (Minneapolis: Fortress, 1992).

A Literary Form and a Way of Speaking

Apocalyptic is both a genre or kind of literature and a type of language that may be used in other genres that are not apocalyptic.

Apocalyptic language uses complex and highly colored metaphors and symbols in order to describe one event in terms of another. In this way, an event can be described and, at the same time, the meaning of the event can be explained.

> We use this kind of language all the time ourselves. Suppose a news reporter had described the fall of the Berlin Wall, as one well might, as an "earth-shattering event." Such a description might perhaps lead some future historian, writing in the *Martian Journal of Early European Studies*, to hypothesize that an earthquake had caused the collapse of the wall, leading to both sides realizing they could live together after all. A good many readings of Daniel or Revelation in our own century operate on about that level of understanding.[5]

Or consider another example, this time five people who are describing the same event. One says, "I was aware of a blur of color and a sudden loud noise." The next says, "I saw and heard a vehicle driving noisily down the road." The next says, "I saw an ambulance on its way to the hospital." The fourth says, "I have just witnessed a tragedy." The fifth says, "This is the end of the world for me." The same event gives rise to five true statements, with each successive one having more "meaning" than the one before. A biblical example of a similar phenomenon occurs in 2 Samuel 18:29–33. David is waiting for news of his troops in the battle against his rebel son Absalom. The first messenger says, "I saw a great commotion, but I do not know what it was." The second says, "May the enemies of my lord the king and all who rise up against you for evil be like that young man." Both have described the same event; the second has invested it with its meaning. Not only, however, has he said what David needed to hear, that

---

5. N. T. Wright, *New Testament and the People of God*, 282–83. The following two paragraphs have been adapted from these pages in Wright's work.

Absalom is dead; he has also invested that news with the further comment, that he himself is a loyal subject of the king. Perhaps he knew the king's inclination for anger against those who brought good but upsetting news (2 Sam. 1:11–16), and chose to give his message obliquely, couching it as an expression of loyalty. David, in turn, makes his own statement about the same event: "O my son Absalom, my son, my son Absalom! Would I had died instead of you, O Absalom, my son, my son!" Each of the speakers is referring to the same event. The different modes of speech invest the reality referred to with increasing layers of meaning.

A Development of Creation Language

Different manners of speaking were available to those who wished to talk or write of the coming day when the covenant God would act to rescue his people. Metaphors from the exodus would come readily to mind, and since the exodus had long been associated with creation itself, metaphors from creation would likewise come to mind. We can understand this better when we bear in mind that Israel believed that the God who had chosen to dwell on the hill called Zion was none other than the Creator of the universe, and that the Holy Land was intended to be the new Eden.

Two examples will make this easy to grasp. The first is from Jeremiah 4. The book of Jeremiah, the biggest and longest of all the major prophets (in terms of words), can be easily summarized in four words: "The Babylonians are coming." Like all other prophets, Jeremiah uses every communicative method to get his message across: plain speech, metaphors, symbols and apocalyptic language, and typology. These different methods are frequently put side by side. First, there is a section where Jeremiah uses plain speech:

Declare in Judah, and proclaim in Jerusalem, and say,

"Blow the trumpet through the land;
   cry aloud and say,

'Assemble, and let us go
    into the fortified cities!'
Raise a standard toward Zion,
    flee for safety, stay not,
for I bring disaster from the north,
    and great destruction.
A lion has gone up from his thicket,
    a destroyer of nations has set out;
    he has gone out from his place
to make your land a waste;
    your cities will be ruins
    without inhabitant.
For this put on sackcloth,
    lament and wail,
for the fierce anger of the LORD
    has not turned back from us." (Jer. 4:5–8 ESV)

In verse 6 God says, "I bring disaster from the north, and great destruction." Anyone who looks at a map will see that Babylon is directly east of Jerusalem. But between Babylon and Jerusalem is a big desert. This is the "D" word. Desert means death. So the only way to get to Jerusalem is to travel up the Euphrates River and come down to Judah and Jerusalem from the north. Therefore the statement, "I bring disaster from the north," means, "The Babylonians are coming to attack you." Admittedly the enemy is described metaphorically as a lion, but in general this brief section is delivered in plain speech.

Later in the chapter, like a good Hebrew, Jeremiah repeats himself. This time he uses apocalyptic language:

I looked on the earth, and behold, it was without form
    and void;
  and to the heavens, and they had no light.
I looked on the mountains, and behold, they were quaking,
    and all the hills moved to and fro.
I looked, and behold, there was no man,

and all the birds of the air had fled.
  I looked, and behold, the fruitful land was a desert,
        and all its cities were laid in ruins
      before the LORD, before his fierce anger. (vv. 23–26 ESV)

Notice carefully what Jeremiah is doing. He is mentally going through the stages of creation described in Genesis 1, and he is reversing them. Chart 6.2 illustrates this.

Chart 6.2

Jeremiah's *Un*-Creation: 4:23–26

Saw	Earth	»	Chaos
	Heavens	»	No Light
Saw	Mountains	»	Quaking
	Hills	»	Shaking
Saw		»	No Man
	Birds	»	Fled
Saw	Fruitful Land	»	Desert
	Cities	»	Ruins

According to the context, however, Jeremiah is predicting the coming of the Babylonians. Since the doctrine of creation is so central to the faith of Israel, he uses the creation account to describe the coming disaster. The destruction brought by the coming of the Babylonians will be an *un*-creation experience. The changes in economic, political, and social life will be so enormous that it will be the end of the world as the people of Israel knew at the time. Nonetheless, he is *not* describing the end of the mass-space-time universe, as in our modern movies. It is apocalyptic language. It is like saying that the fall of the Berlin Wall was an earth-shattering event. It is like the person in the ambulance saying, "This is the end of the world for me."

Another example, both short and simple, is in a section of Isaiah that is, by and large, not apocalyptic at all:

Behold, the day of the LORD comes,
    cruel, with wrath and fierce anger,
to make the land a desolation
    and to destroy its sinners from it.
For the stars of the heavens and their constellations
    will not give their light;
the sun will be dark at its rising,
    and the moon will not shed its light.
I will punish the world for its evil,
    and the wicked for their iniquity;
I will put an end to the pomp of the arrogant,
    and lay low the pompous pride of the ruthless.
        (Isa. 13:9–11 ESV)

Isaiah is predicting future destruction for Babylon. The text is arranged in an A B B′ A′ pattern:

9b	Plain Speech
10a	Apocalyptic Language
10b	Apocalyptic Language
11a	Plain Speech

In plain speech God says he will make the land a desolation (9b) and punish the world for its evil (11a). In between, apocalyptic language is used. Metaphors from creation are employed. The devastation will be an *un*-creation event. We are not supposed to read this literally, as if the moon, sun, and stars will be gone and the mass-space-time universe will no longer exist. No, creation language is reversed to express the gravity of the destruction and change in life brought by this event.

When studying these types of texts, after considering linguistic problems and grasping the vision, we need to identify the historical referent of the vision and then what the symbols are telling us about the historical referent.[6]

---

6. Beale, *Book of Revelation*, 52–53.

Literary Structure

In studying the text, no aspect is harder to grasp than literary structure. It is also difficult to communicate to audiences of today. Expository teaching must be more than communicating the content of the text; we must *explain the form* and show how this carries the meaning.[7] Nowhere is this more important than in apocalyptic.

We can continue to use the book of Daniel to illustrate. On the basis of content, one can easily divide the book of Daniel into six chapters of narratives and four chapters of visions:

Part 1: Six Stories
1. Daniel and Friends in the Court of Babylon
2. King's Dream: The Huge Statue and a Small Stone
3. Daniel's Friends Rescued from a Furnace (Treachery)
4. King's Dream: A Huge Tree (Humbling)
5. Belshazzar and the Writing on the Wall (Humbling)
6. Daniel Rescued from the Lion's Den (Treachery)

Part 2: Four Visions
1. A Vision of Daniel: The Beasts and the Son of Man
2. A Vision of Daniel: The Ram and the Goat
3. A Prayer of Daniel and Vision of the Seventy Weeks
4. A Vision of Daniel: The Book of Truth (about the Future)

Chronological Links

A possible reason for the two-part arrangement of the material in Daniel is chronology. His arrangement, however, is not chronological. In fact, chronology intertwines both parts, since the visions of chapters 7 and 8 occur before the events of chapters 5 and 6.

Linguistic Links

Another possible reason for the two-part arrangement of Daniel is linguistic. The book is bilingual: part is in Hebrew and part in

---

7. See Walter L. Liefeld, *New Testament Exposition: From Text to Sermon* (Grand Rapids, MI: Zondervan, 1984).

Aramaic. However, the linguistic partition does not match the division of stories and visions but rather links the two together.

Literary Links

The two-part arrangement may have been done as an artistic or literary ordering. Here, once again, the arrangement does not follow the division into stories and visions, but matching parts link the two halves together.

So even though the basic division of the book is six chapters of narratives and six chapters of visions, the visions are inextricably linked to the stories in three ways. First, they are linked chronologically. Second, they are linked linguistically. The Aramaic section goes from chapter 2 to chapter 7 and so ties the second half to the first. Third, they are linked structurally. Since the dream of chapter 2 and the vision of chapter 7 are parallel and refer to the same thing, both halves of the book are linked strongly together. The book is a unity and comes from one author. What is the significance of this unity? It is just this: the first half of the book establishes and proves that Daniel has a gift for interpreting dreams and visions in events that could be independently verified by his contemporaries. Therefore, we believe and trust the interpretation of the visions in the second half of the book, which deal with the distant future and hence were not open to verification by the audience of Daniel's time.

In addition, the first six chapters emphasize dominion and authority. The rock cut out from the mountain represents a kingdom that will prevail forever (Dan. 2:44–45); a Babylonian king is forced to confess that God's dominion and kingdom are eternal (Dan. 4:34), as does his son (Daniel 5); and finally a Persian ruler (Dan. 6:26). These great themes form the foundation for the visions and for great preaching today.

The literary structure is the key to both interpretation and teaching. We need a clear view of the whole in order to understand the parts. First, we must see that Daniel 2 and Daniel 7 are about the same thing and are also at the center of the book. Chapter 2 places a gigantic image of man front and center in the Babylonian king's dream. Its head consists of gold, its chest and arms of silver, its belly and thighs of bronze, its legs of iron, and its feet of iron and clay. It is struck down by a rock—cut without hands from a mountain—which then grows to fill the entire earth. The dream foretells four successive human kingdoms succeeded by the kingdom of God, which will endure forever.

Chapter 7 begins the second half of the book in which the Babylonian king's dream is expanded in a series of visions presented like maps with certain sections enlarged. Each successive vision is an enlargement of part of the previous vision; each provides greater and greater detail of the same scene. Daniel replaces the king as dreamer and sees four beasts coming out of the chaotic sea. Then in a picture of the court of heaven, one like a son of man is given the kingdom. The vision of chapter 8 expands on the second and third kingdoms; the vision of chapters 10–12 provides an expanded perspective on events in the third and fourth kingdoms. We now have a road map through the maze. One of my students created a diagram to show this (diagram 6.1[8]). Chapters 2 and 7 give us the basic map, whereas chapters 8, 9, and 10–12 are blowups of parts of the big map.

Diagram 6.1

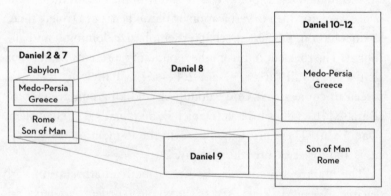

---

8. Jason T. Parry, The Southern Baptist Theological Seminary, personal communication, November 9, 2015.

Interpreting the Symbols

To interpret and teach these sections, we will need to make use of three procedures: (1) *Mining the interpretation sections.* Both chapters 2 and 7 have an interpretation section, which helps us understand the vision. (2) *Comparing Daniel 2 and Daniel 7.* Since chapters 2 and 7 contain the same vision presented in different ways, we can compare and contrast them in our preaching. (3) *Comparing Daniel and Genesis.* The placement of Daniel in the Hebrew Bible invites us to compare and contrast the visions with other parts of the Old Testament. With these three procedures we will deal with Daniel 7, focusing on connections to earlier texts as well as to symbols. We will deal with them in reverse order, because having the larger picture right will help to get the details right.

Comparison of Daniel and Genesis

The books in the Hebrew canon are arranged with prophets and poets between big narrative sections. The prophets and poets are a commentary on the narrative. Thus the arrangement is narrative-commentary-narrative. Daniel is set right at the place where the narrative resumes after the commentary of prophets and poets. This arrangement invites the reader to compare Daniel and Genesis.

There are echoes and reminders of Genesis 1 in the dream of the king in Daniel 2. The dream is really a parody of the divine creation, where God makes humans in the divine likeness to rule the world. Here in Daniel 2, this gigantic figure is made by human hands to rule the world. Pride, the original sin, is at the heart of the earthly kingdoms. A gigantic image destroyed by a small stone also brings to mind another story in Scripture: the confrontation of Goliath by David and the resultant defeat of Goliath with a small stone from the brook. Thus, in Daniel 2, this rock is a Davidic rock, which will grow to be a kingdom without borders.

The first vision, in Daniel 7, also recalls Genesis 1. Instead of a monstrous human image, a parody of the divine image, there is a parody of creation, an anti-creation, if you will! As in Genesis, at the beginning the Spirit or wind blows over the sea. But instead of the creation of light and land, culminating in the divine image, there emerges from the chaotic sea four beasts in succession, each one more horrifying than the previous, until the last one emerges—a macabre spectacle, the embodiment of evil. Each of the beasts is given authority to rule (Dan. 7:6, 12). The final, most bizarre and powerful of the creatures distinguishes itself with the faculty of proud speech, bringing to mind the beast that spoke at the beginning (Dan. 7:7–8; Gen. 3:1–5).

Then the scene shifts from earth to heaven, and a court is sitting with a divine judge on the throne, opening up books and pronouncing a verdict. When the verdict is rendered, the beast on earth is destroyed, and the others are also stripped of their authority. After this scene, an individual like a son of man approaches the divine court in the clouds of heaven, and all power, rule, and honor is given to him. He rules over all the nations, and his kingdom endures forever.

Comparison of Daniel 2 and Daniel 7

The vision of Daniel 7 parallels the dream of Daniel 2 but adds more specific detail. Instead of the gigantic image consisting of four parts, there are four successive beasts, and the divine court and the son of man take the place of the rock that destroys the image. Nebuchadnezzar beheld the kingdoms of this world in terms of a human statue—one single, unified whole. The image was constructed of precious metals, brilliant and dazzling, solid and strong for the most part. In fact, these materials are the most enduring, glorious, and splendid known to man. By contrast, Daniel beholds the kingdoms of this world in terms of animals, ferocious and wild, arising out of an ocean, which is a picture of the chaotic, seething, turbulent mass of humanity. What Daniel sees is an alarming nightmare, full of darkness and terror. The human kingdoms are marked by cruelty, ravenous greed, violence, and inhumanity. It seems that the king's dream gives us the perspective from earth, while Daniel's vision gives the perspective of heaven.

Mining the Interpretation Sections

The beasts from the sea. The beasts appropriately symbolize the four kingdoms. Yet interpreters and preachers frequently devote most of their attention to the identification of the four kingdoms. True, the head in Daniel 2, which corresponds to the lion in chapter 7, is identified as Babylon. In addition, chapter 8, which contains an expansion on the second and third beasts, clearly identifies them as the Medo-Persian and Greek Empires, respectively. The fourth indescribable beast is not named, but Daniel 11:40–45 describes events easily identified as the coming of the Romans in 60 BC–AD 80. Focusing attention on identification of the kingdoms misses much in the text.

Chart 6.3

Comparison of the Four Human Kingdoms and the Kingdom of God

sea (chaos: 7:2)	clouds (order: 7:13)
inhuman	human (7:13)
arrogance (7:8, 11, 20, 25)	humility (7:13, 14)
temporal (7:11, 12, 26, 27)	eternal (7:14, 27)

Contrast the cruelty, ferocity, inhumanity, rapacity, and arrogance against God of human kingdoms and the gracious gift of the eternal kingdom to the holy ones of the Most High. The saints will triumph after a period of suffering; God is in control of history:

a) beast one *humanized* by higher power: 7:4
b) bear *commanded* to devour much meat: 7:5
c) dominion is *given* to four-headed leopard: 7:6
d) fourth beast is *slain* and its body given to the burning of the fire: 7:11
e) remaining three: dominion *taken away*, but extension *granted*: 7:12

The four beasts represent four kingdoms, as in Daniel 2, but the symbolism is more complex. In 7:17 we are told that the four beasts are four kings. In 7:23 the fourth beast is a fourth kingdom. Thus the beast can symbolize a kingdom or the ruler of that kingdom at a particular time. But there is even more. Remember that this is apocalyptic and seeks to describe events and explain the meaning behind the scenes as well. Turn for a moment to Daniel 10:12, 13, and 20. It is clear from these verses that behind an earthly kingdom there is an authority or heavenly power. The messenger speaks to Daniel of the prince of Persia, the prince of Greece, and of Michael, the prince of Israel, who is also one of the chief princes. The idea that there is a heavenly power behind an earthly kingdom is also in Daniel 7. Notice the word *power* (*dominion*, ESV), which occurs seven times in Daniel 7 (vv. 12, 14, 14, 14, 26, 27, 27). In verse 27 we have "the powers." Note that the word occurs in the plural. Just as in the English language, there is a difference between *power* and *powers*, so also in Aramaic. The powers are clearly beings who exercise dominion and power. Thus the animals or beasts represent, first, the power or prince in charge of a kingdom, and then the king over it, and finally the people in it. As we will soon see, the same is true for the son of man, which is a symbol for the heavenly leader as well as the earthly people in the kingdom.

One like a son of man. Just as Daniel describes beasts that are like a lion, like a bear, and like a leopard, so now in verses 13 and 14 he sees one like a son of man coming with the clouds of heaven. Since in the interpretation section the kingdom is given to the "saints of the Most High," many Bible students conclude that the son of man, the individual in the vision who receives all power, is understood to be a corporate expression or collective designation of these saints, who are the people of God, suffering persecution from the fourth beast at the end time.

But is it the case that the son of man is simply a symbol for the people of Israel? It is clear that the four beasts are symbols of four kingdoms, but nowhere does it explicitly state that the son of man is a symbol of the suffering people of God. In the text, what is said is this: Daniel asks for divine insight to understand the meaning of the fourth beast. He is told for the first time that this animal will wage war on everything, including the saints of the Most High, until the divine verdict is pronounced and it receives its death sentence. Moreover, Daniel is told that this beast in particular will specifically challenge God, and God's people will be given into his power for a three and one-half times. After this, the divine verdict will be rendered and the beast destroyed, and the saints will receive the kingship, the power, and the greatness of the kingdom and reign forever and ever.

It is true that these expressions in verses 18, 22, and 27 about the saints being given kingdom and power are also said of the son of man earlier in verse 14, but it may be the case that the son of man has transferred these over to the saints. In other words, the son of man is an individual associated with the saints of the Most High; the connection between the king and his kingdom is the connection between the son of man and the saints. Thus the two are closely identified, but this does not exclude the individuality of the son of man. His destiny is linked to the suffering people of God and vice versa. (The son of man and the saints are closely identified due to the close connection between king and people).

Several things show this to be the correct interpretation. First, in verse 27, the pronouns at the end of the verse are singular and must refer to an individual.

Second, just as the beasts are complex symbols and refer to a heavenly power, an earthly king, and also the kingdom, so also the son of man refers to a heavenly power as well as the earthly kingdom.

Third, the parallel with chapter 2 links the rock and the son of man so that the son of man is a Davidic figure.

Let us look more closely at verses 13 and 14 in the light of the rest of Scripture. Once again, there are clear links to Genesis 1.

The four beasts coming forth from the waters of chaos, rather than through the creative act of God, hearken back to the primal creation in Genesis 1. Rather than being the product of the creative Spirit, they are spawned from the depths of the abyss and are parodies of the divine image. They are savage beasts, manifestations of an archetypal beast, with superhuman strength. In contrast, the son of man is distinctly human and thus extremely weak and insignificant compared to the beasts, with no inherent power or authority. While this figure's name connects him to earth, the fact that he comes on clouds links him to heaven. The coming on clouds suggests an appearance or theophany of Yahweh himself. If Daniel 7:13 does not refer to an appearance of deity, it is the only exception in about seventy instances in the Old Testament. Thus "coming on the clouds of heaven" is a clear indication of deity, while the name "son of man" is a clear indication of humanity. He is given a kingdom, which indicates his royalty. The parallel between the son of man and the rock in chapter 2 shows that the son of man is Davidic.

This passage reflects on the meaning of humans made in the image and likeness of God found in Genesis 1, where human beings are made lords of creation, and everything—including beasts—is put under their feet. Psalm 8 provides a commentary on Genesis and uses the expression "son of man" to describe the exalted position that weak and insignificant humanity has as God's vice president of creation (Ps. 8:4). The term can also be used to designate the Israelite king, God's vice president of Israel, whose fortunes are tied to the nation (Ps. 80:16–19).

Interestingly, in Daniel the son of man does not seek to establish his own authority or to wrest authority through military power or violence but is simply given authority over the world by God. The contrast between the beasts and the son of man is a contrast between a parody of the divine image and the divine image itself, humanity as it was intended to be. That this figure is Davidic is suggested by the parallel with the rock that shattered the gigantic image in chapter 2 and grew to fill the entire earth. His victory will mark the victory of the saints, who will also be given authority and dominion over the entire world. Humanity will regain the dominion and royal status conferred on it at the beginning.

7

Describing the Future, Part 3

The Already and the Not Yet

The Bible is a divine-human book. It was written by humans; it claims at the same time to be the word of God. This is clearly stated by the apostle Peter specifically in regard to the biblical prophets:

> . . . knowing this first of all, that no prophecy of Scripture comes from someone's own interpretation. For no prophecy was ever produced by the will of man, but men spoke from God as they were carried along by the Holy Spirit (2 Pet. 1:20–21 ESV)

Men, moved by the Holy Spirit, spoke from God. Although there are different kinds of revelation, as Hebrews 1:1 states, and we cannot always distinguish the divine and human elements, one aspect of the human side of things is clear: the human authors who wrote the words were *always* deeply meditating and thinking upon passages of Scripture written before their time.

It is not surprising, then, that books composed later actually cite passages from books written earlier or allude to them in a variety of ways. For example, Isaiah derives his doctrine of future salvation from the biblical teaching on creation in the book of Genesis. This is clear in Isaiah 40. Since there is one creator God, and this God is in covenant with Israel, why should we think that God doesn't know about the condition of his people or is unable and unwilling to help? This is the argument he presents there. It also seems likely that his teaching about future judgment, whether of Israel (e.g., 6:13) or of unbelievers (66:24), as fire is derived from the revelation of Yahweh at Sinai as a burning fire (Exodus 3 and 19, cf. Genesis 15). Zechariah, a book coming at the end of the Old Testament, has four passages about a shepherd that appear to be based on the four songs about the servant in Isaiah.

Use in the New Testament

The idea that later writers of Scripture help to interpret earlier writers of Scripture means that citations of the prophets by later writers of the Old and New Testaments are important in learning how to read and understand the biblical prophets. This is especially true if we want to have a *Christian* understanding of the prophets. If all we are doing is exegesis based on the cultural setting of the text, the linguistic data, and the literary structure, what would make our exegesis Christian as opposed, for example, to Jewish or other scholarly study of these texts? The answer is that if we do not listen to the teaching of Jesus and the apostles in the New Testament, our understanding of the biblical prophets is not a *Christian interpretation*, no matter how skilled we are in the details of exegesis!

With the first coming of Jesus, we learn from him and his authorized agents, the apostles, that there is an already and not yet to the fulfillment of the prophecies given in the Old Testament. Consider a couple of examples to illustrate this.

In Luke 4:16–21, Jesus quotes Isaiah 61:1–3 and comments on the fulfillment of the prophecy. Both passages need to be given here in full:

The Spirit of the Lord GOD is upon me,
 because the LORD has anointed me
to bring good news to the poor;
 he has sent me to bind up the brokenhearted,
to proclaim liberty to the captives,
 and the opening of the prison to those who are bound;
to proclaim the year of the LORD's favor,
 and the day of vengeance of our God;
 to comfort all who mourn;
to grant to those who mourn in Zion—
 to give them a beautiful headdress instead of ashes,
the oil of gladness instead of mourning,
 the garment of praise instead of a faint spirit;
that they may be called oaks of righteousness,
 the planting of the LORD, that he may be glorified.
They shall build up the ancient ruins;
 they shall raise up the former devastations;
they shall repair the ruined cities,
 the devastations of many generations. (Isa. 61:1–4 ESV)

And he came to Nazareth, where he had been brought up. And as was his custom, he went to the synagogue on the Sabbath day, and he stood up to read. And the scroll of the prophet Isaiah was given to him. He unrolled the scroll and found the place where it was written,

 "The Spirit of the Lord is upon me,
  because he has anointed me
   to proclaim good news to the poor.
 He has sent me to proclaim liberty to the captives
  and recovering of sight to the blind,
   to set at liberty those who are oppressed,
 to proclaim the year of the Lord's favor."

And he rolled up the scroll and gave it back to the attendant and sat down. And the eyes of all in the synagogue were fixed on him. And he began to say to them, "Today this Scripture has been fulfilled in your hearing." (Luke 4:16–21 ESV)

Notice that when Jesus reads from Isaiah 61, he stops in the middle of verse 19. He does not read, ". . . and the day of vengeance of our God," although versification could well have been marked in the scroll from which he was reading (as we see in the Masada Psalms scroll). Why is this? It is because he has come to proclaim the year of emancipation and Jubilee release, but the judgment will have to wait until his second coming. This is not the time of judgment, when all wrongs will be righted.

What Isaiah the prophet didn't know and see in the vision he was reporting to Judah on behalf of Yahweh is that there would be a gap of at least two thousand years between the first half of the verse and the second half.

In diagram 7.1, there are two mountains separated by a valley.

Diagram 7.1

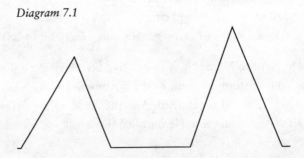

As Isaiah looks at the coming of the King/Messiah, he is looking from the left toward the right and sees both mountains as one. Only when we look at it from the side do we see that there are actually two mountains with a valley between. This is the perspective of the writers of the New Testament, who have the benefit of understanding that there is a first and a second coming of the Messiah. His first coming is in grace; his second coming is in judgment. Isaiah sees only one mountain and puts the grace and judgment together in one breath.

A similar thing happens when the New Testament writers interpret Zechariah 12:10:

> And I will pour out on the house of David and the inhabitants of Jerusalem a spirit of grace and pleas for mercy, so that, when they look on me, on him whom they have pierced, they shall mourn for him, as one mourns for an only child, and weep bitterly over him, as one weeps over a firstborn. (ESV)

This passage is cited twice in the New Testament as follows:

> But one of the soldiers pierced his side with a spear, and at once there came out blood and water. He who saw it has borne witness—his testimony is true, and he knows that he is telling the truth—that you also may believe. For these things took place that the Scripture might be fulfilled: "Not one of his bones will be broken." And again another Scripture says, "They will look on him whom they have pierced." (John 19:34–37 ESV)

> Behold, he is coming with the clouds, and every eye will see him, even those who pierced him, and all tribes of the earth will wail on account of him. Even so. Amen. (Rev. 1:7 ESV)

In Zechariah 12:10 Yahweh is speaking. He says they will look upon him, whom they pierced, and mourn for him as one mourns for an only child. The apostle John sees the first half of the verse fulfilled in the crucifixion of Jesus. This is when Yahweh, or the Lord, was pierced. According to Revelation 1:7, the tribes of the earth will mourn or wail at the second coming of Jesus. So the first half of Zechariah 12:10 is fulfilled at the first coming, and the second half will be fulfilled at the second coming.

Two citations in Matthew are similar. In Matthew 24:30 Jesus combines Zechariah 12:10 and Daniel 7:13 to present a picture of the Messiah, who establishes a kingdom through suffering. In Matthew 26:64 Jesus combines Psalm 110 and Daniel 7:13 to portray the Messiah as the ruler coming to reign over the earth in a universal, worldwide, everlasting kingdom. This occurs after a period of struggle on the earth, which is what we see in Daniel 7:21–22. So Matthew also sees Zechariah 12:10 as being fulfilled in both the first coming and the second coming of Jesus.

Already and Not Yet

As is well known in biblical theology, the kingdom of Jesus Christ has been inaugurated but not consummated. There is an already as well as a not yet that applies to his kingdom. According to the New Testament, the kingdom of God is already and not yet. Nonetheless, the prophets of the Old Testament put everything together in one grand picture and do not clearly distinguish the first and second comings of the Messiah.

This principle means that we cannot construct a chronology of events from the prophets of the Old Testament concerning the coming of the King and the coming of his kingdom. We need the teaching of Jesus and the apostles to clarify which prophecies apply to the first coming and which apply to the second coming. It is even possible that some prophecies can apply to both at the same time.

Conclusion

I have been planning for some time to write this brief work. For me personally, many years of study have been necessary to begin to accurately articulate and describe how Hebrew literature and, in particular, the writings of the prophets are to be read and understood.

In 2015 Aaron Chalmers published a similar work entitled *Interpreting the Prophets: Reading, Understanding, and Preaching from the Worlds of the Prophets.*[1] Chalmers's book is slightly more academic than this one. He devotes attention to defining what a prophet is, to describing the historical world of the prophets, their rhetorical and theological world, and the subtle shift from prophecy to apocalyptic writings. I would suggest that his helpful work is complementary to the one I have written.

One interesting commonality of our books is how each compares reading the literature of the prophets to reading comics, and this happened independently.

My book focuses much more on how Hebrew literature works and how it differs from the kind of literature we are familiar with in the Western world. In the past one hundred years and more, Christians have hotly debated eschatology—what the Bible teaches about future events. The biggest problem in all this is that we have not known the rules and strategies used by the biblical

---

1. Aaron Chalmers, *Interpreting the Prophets: Reading, Understanding, and Preaching from the Worlds of the Prophets* (Downers Grove, IL: IVP Academic, 2015).

prophets for communication, and we do not understand the texts they have written.

The debate between literal interpretation and spiritual interpretation is entirely bogus. When the Reformers talked about the "literal sense" of the text, they meant the meaning intended by author *according to the rules of the genre of literature* being used to communicate the message. Listen to the prophets themselves. Hosea, one of the earliest writing prophets, says this:

> I spoke to the prophets,
>   gave them many visions
>   and told parables through them. (Hos. 12:10 NIV)

Here we are reminded that God communicated to the prophets not only by visions but also by parables. Note how all Jesus's parables begin with the statement "The kingdom of God *is like* . . ." So the prophets are actually telling us: "Pay attention! We are using symbols and types when we speak."

I have attempted to describe and spell out the communicative methods used by the biblical prophets. Most people in the Western world will have to consciously apply these principles before they can read and understand the biblical prophets the way they turn from the front page of the newspaper to read the comics.

Appendix

Literary Structure of the
Book of Revelation

The way in which an author *arranges* his statements and structures his thoughts contributes significantly to the communication as a whole. In fact, perhaps as much as *50 percent* of the meaning in a text is communicated by the literary shape of the text and not by any single proposition or statement in the text. Sadly, this is not reflected in many commentaries. The heritage of the Enlightenment period has contributed to an atomistic study of the text, focusing on minute details of grammar and the meanings of words and neglecting the perspective given by the structure of the text as a whole.

Here I wish to briefly describe the literary structure of the book of Revelation as analyzed by Andrew M. Fountain.[1] There is a wide variety of interpretations of the book of Revelation. Many interpretations in the last one hundred years have not understood that while John is writing in Greek, this book follows the characteristics of the Hebrew prophets. When we combine this fact with an understanding of the literary structure, we will be able to grasp *clearly* and *simply* what the book communicates.

---

1. See http://chri.st/structure-revelation.

Revelation: Seven Sequences of Seven

Prologue: Vision of Jesus Christ among the candlesticks [1]

1. Seven Letters to the Churches [2 & 3]

2:1–7 Ephesus	2:8–11 Smyrna	2:12–17 Pergamum	2:18–29 Thyatira

Introduction: The Lamb is worthy to open the seals [4 & 5]   **The First Scroll**

2. Seals [6–8:1]

6:1–2 White horse: conqueror	6:3–4 Red horse: war	6:5–6 Black horse: famine & oppression	6:7–8 Pale horse: death by sword, famine & disease

3. Seven Trumpets [8:2–11] Prologue [8:2–6]
  Offering up of the prayers of the faithful

8:7 Earth damaged	8:8–9 Sea damaged	8:10–11 Rivers damaged	8:12 Sun damaged

4. Seven Visions of Warfare [12–14]   **The Second Scroll**

12:1–2 Woman with crown of 12 stars	12:3–6 Huge Red Dragon	12:7–18 War in heaven: Dragon thrown down to earth	13:1–10 Beast from the sea

5. Seven Final Plagues [15–16] Prologue [15:1–16:1]
  Offering up of the worship of the faithful

16:2 Earth plague	16:3 Sea plague	16:4–7 River plague	16:8–9 Sun plague

6. Seven Visions of Victory [17–19]

17 The Great Prostitute (Babylon)	18 The Fall of Babylon	19:1–5 Vast throng in heaven praise God for judgements	19:6–10 Vast throng in heaven announce the wedding of the Lamb
		HALLELUJAH!	

7. Seven Visions of the End of the Age and the New Creation [20–22:5]

20:1–6 The Dragon: subdued for 1000 years	20:7–10 The Dragon: released, fights, and is thrown into lake of fire	20:11–15 Great white throne. The dead are judged	21:1 A new heaven and a new earth
			WOW!

Epilogue [22:6–21] I am coming soon!

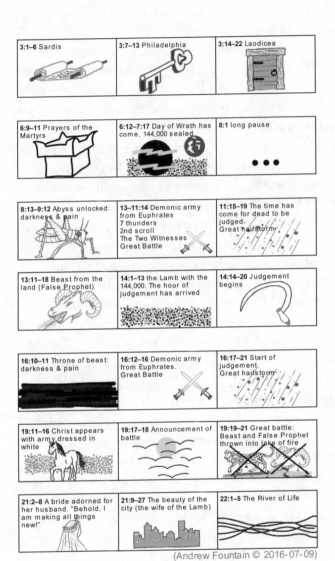

3:1–6 Sardis	3:7–13 Philadelphia	3:14–22 Laodicea
6:9–11 Prayers of the Martyrs	6:12–7:17 Day of Wrath has come, 144,000 sealed	8:1 long pause
8:13–9:12 Abyss unlocked: darkness & pain	13–11:14 Demonic army from Euphrates 7 thunders 2nd scroll The Two Witnesses Great Battle	11:15–19 The time has come for dead to be judged. Great hailstorm
13:11–18 Beast from the land (False Prophet)	14:1–13 the Lamb with the 144,000. The hour of judgement has arrived	14:14–20 Judgement begins
16:10–11 Throne of beast: darkness & pain	16:12–16 Demonic army from Euphrates. Great Battle	16:17–21 Start of judgement. Great hailstorm
19:11–16 Christ appears with army dressed in white	19:17–18 Announcement of battle	19:19–21 Great battle: Beast and False Prophet thrown into lake of fire
21:2–8 A bride adorned for her husband. "Behold, I am making all things new!"	21:9–27 The beauty of the city (the wife of the Lamb)	22:1–5 The River of Life

(Andrew Fountain © 2016-07-09)

Andrew Fountain provides the chart, reproduced in this appendix, to help visualize the literary structure. The chart can be explained simply in just a few steps.

First, note that Revelation consists of seven large sections, each consisting of seven paragraphs or smaller sections. Part of this is obvious. There are seven letters to the churches, there are seven seals, there are seven trumpets, and there are seven bowls or plagues. This is a big clue from the author. The division of the three remaining sections into seven smaller divisions is fairly obvious from the text and need not be defended at length here.

Second, note that the book comes in two scrolls or volumes. Chapters 4 and 5 introduce the reader to a first scroll having seven seals. From this scroll come fourteen paragraphs describing seven seals and seven trumpets. Then in 9:13–11:14, toward the end of the sequence of trumpets, we learn of another small scroll, which John is to "eat." It will be sweet in his mouth but bitter in his stomach (10:1–2, 8–11). From the second scroll come the remaining four sequences of seven paragraphs. A bolded line in the chart indicates the division of Revelation into two volumes. The judgments in volume 2 are painted in brighter colors, with more vivid allegory in volume 1.

Third, both the second and the fourth sequence (the seven seals, and the seven visions of warfare) begin with the ascension of Jesus after his resurrection and end with judgment. This suggests that these two sequences are chronologically parallel.

A brief explanation is needed to demonstrate the meaning of 6:1–2 and 12:1–2. In 6:1–2 we have a picture of a conqueror on a white horse. This seems to be parallel to 19:11, and I interpret this as Jesus Christ. This is disputed, since Beale believes it is the Antichrist.[2] Consider the following background in the Old Testament. In Exodus 15:3 the Lord is called a "man of war." This is an unusual title given to Yahweh, given to him in only one other place:

---

2. G. K. Beale, *The Book of Revelation*, New International Greek Testament Commentary (Grand Rapids, MI: Eerdmans, 1999), 375–77.

Isaiah 42:13. The use in Isaiah belongs to the fact that he is using the language of God's great deliverance in the past to describe a future salvation. In other words, Isaiah 42:13 is consciously using the term as new-exodus language. This idea is developed further in Psalms 2 and 110. In Psalm 2 the nations revolt against Yahweh and his Davidic king. God laughs and gives the nations to the Davidic king as his inheritance. This future descendent of David will "rule them with an iron scepter and dash them to pieces like pottery" (v. 9). This imagery carries forward the picture of a ruler who is a warrior. Psalm 23 may be the favorite psalm in America, but Psalm 110 is the favorite of the early church, since it is quoted more than any other psalm in the New Testament. It divides into two stanzas. A declaration from Yahweh creates a king in the first stanza who is commanded to sit at the footstool of God's throne until God makes him rule over all his enemies. An oath in the second stanza creates a priest, and, strangely, this priest is a real warrior:

> The Lord is at your right hand;
>> he will shatter kings on the day of his wrath.
> He will execute judgment among the nations,
>> filling them with corpses;
> he will shatter the chief
>> over a big country.
> He will drink from the brook by the way;
>> therefore he will lift up his head. (Ps. 110:5–7)

The future king conquers the nations! Note that the rider on the white horse in Revelation 19:11 is clearly a reference to Jesus Christ, but apparently this is not persuasive for Beale.

The authors of the New Testament cite Psalm 110 because they believed this began to be fulfilled at the ascension of Jesus Christ to heaven. This is when he sat down at the right hand of the throne of God and began to extend his mighty scepter from Zion. Every time someone puts their faith in Jesus Christ, folks from the enemy nations are conquered and brought into the kingdom of Jesus. This is why we see Revelation 6:1–2 as marking the ascension.

Interpretation of Revelation 12:1–9 is easier. We have a sign, i.e., a prophetic, symbolic vision: a woman clothed with the sun, with the moon under her feet, and a crown of twelve stars on her head. This reminds us of Joseph's dreams. The woman represents Israel. She is about to give birth to a male child who is obviously the Messiah or coming King since he will "rule all the nations with an iron scepter" (v. 5), an obvious allusion to Psalm 2. The male child is caught up to heaven, a clear reference to the ascension, and the woman is whisked away to the desert. This is the new Israel on the new-exodus journey through the desert toward the Promised Land.

Since sequences 2 and 4 both begin with the ascension and end with the judgment, they represent the current age between the first and second comings of Christ.

Fourth, note that sequences 3 and 5 are precisely parallel: the first paragraph damages the earth, the second damages the sea, the third damages the rivers, the fourth damages the sun, the fifth unlocks darkness and pain, the sixth brings a demonic army from the Euphrates, and the seventh entails a great hailstorm. Here, in typical Hebrew fashion, the author repeats descriptions of a sequence of great judgments.

The parallel sequences in 2 / 4 and 3 / 5 are connected in 7:1–4 as follows:

> After this I saw four angels standing at the four corners of the earth, holding back the four winds of the earth, that no wind might blow on earth or sea or against any tree. Then I saw another angel ascending from the rising of the sun, with the seal of the living God, and he called with a loud voice to the four angels who had been given power to harm earth and sea, saying, "Do not harm the earth or the sea or the trees, until we have sealed the servants of our God on their foreheads." And

I heard the number of the sealed, 144,000, sealed from every tribe of the sons of Israel. (ESV)

Carefully observe that the angels may not harm the land and the sea until the full number of the servants of God is sealed. The harming of the land and the sea is a clear reference to sequences 3 and 5. So these sequences are blowups or expansions of the sixth and seventh seals. It seems that the book of Revelation has a literary structure like that of Daniel. There are sections giving an overview and sections providing blowups of parts of the overview.

Fifth, the seven visions of warfare in sequence 4 and the seven visions of victory in sequence 6 are in chiastic arrangement: in sequence four we have (1) dragon, (2) beast and false prophet, and (3) Babylon fallen (Rev. 14:1–13). In sequence 6 (and beginning of 7) we have the exact reverse: (3) Babylon fallen, (2) beast and false prophet, and (1) dragon. So we conclude that sequences 6 and 7 are a blowup or expansion of the judgments at the end of the sixth and seventh seals in sequence 4.

The seventh and final sequence is the only sequence that does not end in judgment. The judgment is described in paragraph 3, and after that we have the new creation, the new people of God, the new city of God, and the river of life.

The arrangement in the last sequence suggests that this sequence is a quick overview of everything from the beginning of the church to the age of the new creation. Therefore, the first paragraph, Revelation 20:1–6, would be a quick summary of the period between the first and second coming of Christ, at least up to the time of the Antichrist and terrible tribulation. Probably the beast, false prophet, and dragon are all manifestations of the same evil opponent of God. Those who die for the cause of Christ live (the verb says "live," not "come to life") and reign with Christ. They live because all who put faith and trust in Jesus Christ are a new creation (spiritually). Unless they are alive at the coming of Christ, they must face death and be raised from the dead. Putting faith in Christ would be the first resurrection (spiritual), and being raised would be the second resurrection (physical).

The opposite is the case for unbelievers. Since they have no first resurrection, they experience physical death and then spiritual death in the lake of fire. "This is the second death," says John. Revelation 20:1–6 is a tremendous motivation to evangelism. At the cross, Jesus has gone into the strong man's house and bound the strong man (Satan). Now is the time when people can be freed from the house and kingdom of Satan. Later when the Antichrist is in full force, this will not be possible, because the number of God's servants will be sealed at that time.

One of my classmates at seminary claims that because the words "one thousand" are repeated six times, we must understand them as a literal one thousand years. This is a major error in interpretation. It is like insisting that we read the comics as we read the front page of the newspaper. It is like claiming that because clouds occur in six out of seven cartoon frames, they are literal clouds and not symbolic of coming storms.

Note that the basic sequence of events provided in Revelation according to the literary structure and the interpretation given here agrees with the teaching of Jesus (Matthew 24) and Paul (2 Thessalonians 2). An historic premillennial position might also work with the literary structure of the text as presented by Andrew Fountain.

General Index

Abrahamic covenant, 16, 53, 60, 66, 76; fulfillment of, 65
Absalom, 101–2
Ahaz, 19, 52
Amos, 59, 99
Anderson, Bernhard W., 75, 79
angels, 71, 98, 130–31
Antichrist, 128
antiphonal singing, 86
Arabia, oracle concerning, 96–97
Aristotle, 42
Assyria, 19, 35, 36, 64, 69, 70; and the conquest of Judah, 37–38

Baal, 16
Babylon, 36, 38–39, 53, 76–77, 78, 79, 80–81, 95, 96–97, 103, 105, 111; oracle concerning, 66
Basic Forms of Prophetic Speech (Westermann), 15
Bathsheba, 19
Beale, G. K., 128, 129
Bible, the, 14, 17, 41, 75; descriptions of the court of heaven in, 71–72; as a divine-human book, 117; key theme of, 94; narrative plot structure of, 90–91, 91n9; and the placement of Daniel in, 109. *See also* literature, apocalyptic; literature, Hebrew

biblical prophets. *See* Old Testament prophets
Book of the Twelve, 59

Canaan, 88–89
Chalmers, Aaron, 123
comics, 11–12
covenants: covenant curses, 63–64; covenant relationships, 16n2; and the plot structure of the Bible, 91n9. *See also* Abrahamic covenant; Davidic covenant; Mosaic covenant
Cyrus, 35, 36

Damascus, 19, 96
Daniel, book of, 97–98. *See also* Daniel, book of, interpreting the symbols in; Daniel, book of, two-part literary structure of
Daniel, book of, interpreting the symbols in, 109; and the comparison of Daniel 2 and Daniel 7, 110–11; and the comparison of Daniel and Genesis, 109–10; interpreting the beasts from the sea, 111–12, 114; interpreting the one like a son of man, 112–15
Daniel, book of, two-part literary structure of, 106; chronological

Scripture Index

A Concise Overview of God's Covenants

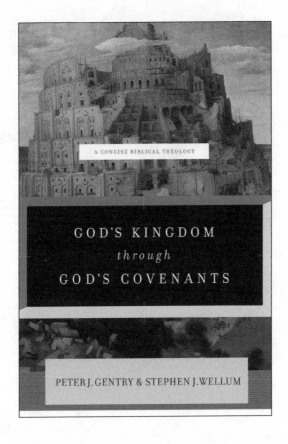

This book introduces readers to the biblical covenants, charting a middle course between dispensationalism and covenant theology. It is an accessible and abridged version of the influential theological work *Kingdom through Covenant*.

crossway.org